Keep Thy heart with All diligence
For out of it flow the springs
Of Life. Proverb 4 : 23

100
MEDITATIONS
FOR
ADVENT AND
CHRISTMAS

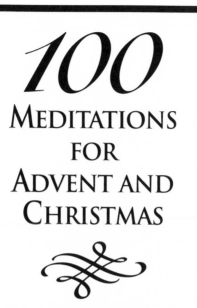

100 MEDITATIONS FOR ADVENT AND CHRISTMAS

SELECTED FROM

The Upper Room Daily Devotional Guide

UPPER ROOM BOOKS

NASHVILLE

Scripture quotations designated NRSV are from the New Revised
Standard Version of the Bible, copyright © 1989 by the Division of
Christian Education, National Council of the Churches of Christ in
the United States, and are used by permission.

Scripture quotations designated NIV are from the *Holy Bible, New
International Version.* Copyright © 1973, 1978, 1984 International
Bible Society. Used by permission of Zondervan Bible Publishers.

Scripture quotations designated NASB are taken from the *New
American Standard Bible,* © 1960, 1962, 1963, 1968, 1971, 1972, 1973,
1975, 1977 by The Lockman Foundation. Used by permission.

Scripture quotations designated TEV are from the *Good News
Bible,* The Bible in Today's English Version-Old Testament: Copy-
right © American Bible Society 1976; New Testament: Copyright ©
American Bible Society 1966, 1971, 1976.

Scripture quotations designated RSV are from the Revised Standard Version of the Bible, copyright 1946, 1952, and © 1971 by the
Division of Christian Education, National Council of the Churches
of Christ in the USA, and are used by permission.

The designation KJV identifies quotations from the King James
Version of the Bible.

Cover illustration: NATIVITY, serigraph, Image size: 38" x 11" ©
1988 John August Swanson, Los Angeles artist. Courtesy of
Bergsma Gallery, Grand Rapids MI.
First Printing: August 1994 (10)
ISBN: 0-8358-0707-X
Library of Congress Catalog Card Number: 94-60657

Contents

———— ~ ————

Introduction

WALKING THE EARTH SINGING

———— ~ ————

WE HAVE LEFT THE CAMP SINGING was the message
written on a postcard pushed between the boards of
the cattle car full of Jewish prisoners on their way from
Westerbork in the Netherlands to the gas chambers of
Auschwitz. Etty Hillesum, a young Jewish woman
who had developed a remarkable relationship with
God as she served the other prisoners and awaited
certain death, wrote those words. She could have been
fearful, sullen, angry, despondent, hopeless, and des-
pairing. But she was not because she saw beyond, and
perhaps through, the horrors of her world to another and
greater reality where God's reign of love, justice,
mercy, and peace overcame the illusions of this world.

Luke records Mary's song that describes a similar
reality of love, justice, mercy, and peace. In her song,
which Luke records in chapter 1, Mary outlines the

good news that Jesus embodied and brought to the world. We remind one another of this good news during Advent and Christmas. We remember that the full reign of God will overthrow and replace the false reality of hatred, greed, corruption, and war. Our remembrance is the transforming Christmas story we love to hear and desire to tell to all the world.

But our world, like Mary's and Etty's, has its darker and shadowed side. Therefore, we remind one another of the truth of this transforming story to strengthen and uphold our lives. We encourage one another to walk the earth singing because we know that the illusions of this world are giving way to the reality of God's reign of love, justice, mercy, peace, and goodness. These scripture readings, meditations, and prayers can help us leave the world of illusion behind and live in the real world of God's reign and presence, even today.

~Rueben P. Job
Grandfather of Sam, Will, and Laura
Husband of Beverly
Bishop, retired

WAITING

1 CHRISTMAS POSSIBILITIES
Read Luke 1:39-56

When you were young, you used to get ready and go anywhere you wanted to; but when you are old, you will stretch out your hands and someone else will tie you up and take you where you don't want to go.

—John 21:18 (TEV)

IN HER SONG OF PRAISE, MARY epitomizes one who has opened herself totally to God's will. Such complete willingness to be used in God's plan is foreign to many of us today. We emphasize personal achievement, individual satisfaction, strike-first capability, taking control and staying in control. With these emphases, how do we open ourselves to God's new order? How do we become pregnant with the wonderful possibilities that God revealed to us nearly 2,000 years ago and keeps prodding us with at each celebration of Jesus' birth? How can we proclaim with integrity the angels' message—"Glory to God in the highest, and on earth peace and good will to all"?

Let us, like Mary, surrender control of ourselves to God's will. Let our response to Christmas possibilities grow. Then we, like Peter, will be willing to go where we do not want to go.

Prayer: God, we ask ourselves: Are we ready for Christmas possibilities? Can we surrender control? We wait for Your guidance. Amen.

THOUGHT FOR THE DAY
Can we sing Mary's song this Christmas?
~Janet R. Knight (Tennessee)

2 ANSWERED PRAYER
Read 2 Kings 5:8-17

Whatsoever we ask, we receive of him, because we keep his commandments, and do those things that are pleasing in his sight.
—1 John 3:22 (KJV)

"How boring! Why do I have to go?" asked Scott.

Looking at Christmas lights in another part of the city was a waste of time to our teenage son. He didn't know that we were actually picking up a very special present, the golden retriever pup he had wanted for years. He finally agreed to go. If he had continued to refuse, he would have missed a very happy surprise. It reminded me of Naaman, who almost missed receiving his healing because he didn't want to do what God had instructed through the prophet Elisha.

Just like Scott and Naaman, I often come close to missing God's blessings. God's ways sometimes seem strange to me. I ask God for an improved relationship, and God asks me to swallow my pride and extend kindness to someone who has been unkind to me. I ask God for forgiveness, and God commands that I forgive the one who has hurt me. I ask for success, and God brings me great lessons through rejection and failure. I must realize that the answer to my prayer lies in my obedience to the Lord. There is no other way.

Prayer: Lord Jesus, make me willing to obey You. Amen.

THOUGHT FOR THE DAY
Answers to prayer depend upon our obedience.

~Ann Lunde (Oregon)

3 SOAKING IN GOD'S WORD
Read Psalm 119:9-16

Their delight is in the law of the LORD, and on his law they meditate day and night.

—Psalm 1:2 (NRSV)

MY LIFE HAD BECOME EXTREMELY BUSY. Pressures of work piled up. I went to bed exhausted and woke up tired. Doing routine household tasks became an irritation. I felt resentful of any new demands on my time.

Finally Christmas came, and I had a few days off. One day I decided to take a long, soaking bath. As I sat in the tub, enjoying those solitary moments, I realized that it had been months since I had done this. My quick, two-minute morning showers could not equal the refreshment of these moments of relaxing in the hot water.

A few weeks earlier I had realized that my priorities had gotten out of order. God was no longer first or even second on my list. As I relaxed in the tub, I understood why.

My quick "Good morning, God," prayers had not sufficed to refresh my spirit. They, and the few verses of scripture I would read occasionally, had been like the two-minute showers, something that I had done but with no joy in the doing.

A long, soaking bath in God's word and in God's presence was long overdue and needed to become a regular part of my life. I needed to rediscover delight in the Bible.

Prayer: Teach me Your ways, O Lord, for You are the God of my salvation. Amen.

THOUGHT FOR THE DAY
Is it time for you to soak yourself in God's Word?

~Diann B. Lopez (Arizona)

4 NOT JUST YET
Read Mark 13:32-37

"Surely I am coming soon." Amen. Come, Lord Jesus!
—Revelation 22:20 (RSV)

WHEN MY CHILDREN WERE YOUNG, the floor of their playroom often became messy with games and toys strewn everywhere. Every now and again I would say, "I'm going round the corner to the shop. When I come back, everything should be in its place." I would give each child a task—the more complicated tasks to the older ones, the very simplest to the youngest. Then I would leave.

When I returned, sometimes I would come quietly up the stairs and see through the half-open door that they were quarreling or fooling around or just absorbed in something. Then I might creep away to give them another chance. Sometimes I would shut the front door with a bang and hear sudden noises of bustle as they hurried to get the room straightened. Inevitably one would call out, "Not just yet, Mummy. Give us a little longer."

Each Advent I recall this experience with my children and wonder how many times the Lord has been close at hand, seeing the chaos of our world and longing to come, but waiting, sparing us judgment a little longer. We love God—but not enough to be ready, not just yet.

Prayer: Move our hearts, Lord, with such love for You that we will be ready, daily, to look upon You, face to face. Amen.

THOUGHT FOR THE DAY
The Lord is near at hand.
~Prudence Phillipson (Northumberland, England)

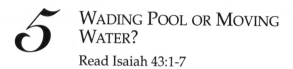

5 WADING POOL OR MOVING WATER?

Read Isaiah 43:1-7

"My thoughts are not your thoughts, neither are your ways my ways," declares the LORD.

—Isaiah 55:8 (NIV)

WALKING BY THE RIVER one spring day, I came upon three of my neighbor's pet geese flailing about in the river's swollen waters. They could not go back to where they had gotten in, but they were struggling to remain in the calm inlet. If they were pulled into the main current, they would be swept rapidly downstream. After a few minutes, the geese stopped struggling and the current whisked them away. All three pets safely floated downriver, got out at a calmer spot, and waddled home to safety. The rushing water that appeared to be a calamity actually turned out to be the way home for the geese.

Often we prefer to remain in safe and familiar waters rather than risk the turbulence of growth and change. Yet calm waters can also be stagnant. God leads us to fresher, smoother currents, but sometimes we must go into turbulent waters to find them. At times when God is encouraging us toward change, our resistance can be what creates the turmoil that so frightens us. In caring concern, God gently urges us to relax and see where openness to change will take us.

Prayer: God, we thank You for Your presence in the wading pools as well as the whirlpools of life. Your love never falls. Amen.

THOUGHT FOR THE DAY

If God is urging you into turbulent waters, you can be sure you will not enter them alone.

~Beverly Naleway (New Hampshire)

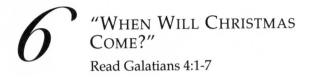

6 "WHEN WILL CHRISTMAS COME?"

Read Galatians 4:1-7

The people that walked in darkness have seen a great light: they that dwell in the land of the shadow of death upon them hath the light shined

—Isaiah 9:2 (KJV)

WALKING near a store window, we heard a small boy ask his mother, "When will Christmas come?" Who among us does not count the days until Christmas?

The answer to this question began in the heart and mind of God in the quiet, unbroken calm of eternity. The world began, the human race stumbled and fell, kings and princes rose into glory and fell into dust—and then one day God placed the Child in a manger and changed the course of the world. This Child is our hope, in Him is our faith.

As Christmas comes now, we must know that He alone can make the world a better world. Christ is the world's Savior. Christ alone can reply to the question of our childlike hearts, "When will Christmas come?" This is the reassuring answer: "It came with Jesus' birth. He has brought everything we need, everything we have asked of God. Christmas is God's gift of eternal joy and hope and peace to all everywhere."

Prayer: The world will ever be thanking Thee, O God, as we do this day, for the night Christ was born. May Thy eternal gift reside within us. In His name we praise Thee. Amen.

THOUGHT FOR THE DAY

Mary had implicit faith in God's way of working wonders. So must we.

~Raymond M. Veh (Thiensville, Wisconsin)

7 WHO IS INDISPENSABLE?
Read Psalm 6

Give me strength; I am completely exhausted and my whole being is deeply troubled.

—Psalm 6:2-3 (TEV)

IT HAPPENED IN A SPLIT SECOND. There I was, lying on the icy ground, unable to move. With someone's help I was able to get up, but my left arm was numb. I was in a town that had no doctor, and it was hours later that I was able to get medical attention. My arm was broken just below the shoulder. It would take six to eight weeks to heal.

Chaos reigned within me. What was I to do? I was a busy woman. I had made commitments and appointments and did not want to disappoint anyone. But I had no choice. For two weeks I was on medical leave, helpless and in considerable pain. During that time friends stepped forward—taking on my responsibilities, aiding me to get dressed and fed. Eventually, I was able to drive and go to work. Life returned to normal.

I learned much during those weeks. I learned that I am not indispensable, that I can be patient, that I need to ask for help. But most of all I learned that there are those who care, who are willing to go the extra mile to show their love and concern. I discovered that God is truly present in my life through others.

Prayer: Dear God, help us to remember that we all need each other. Amen.

THOUGHT FOR THE DAY
In suffering, we discover our hidden strengths.

~Loretta Girzaitis (Minnesota)

8 MORE THAN HALFWAY
Read Revelation 22:16-21

Even so, come, Lord Jesus.
—Revelation 22:20 (KJV)

WHEN TAKING FAREWELL of Syrian congregations in Iraq and Iran, I noticed that the people never said good-bye. Instead they said, *"Maranatha"*—"O Lord, come!"

Laden with *Maranatha*, the season of Advent celebrates the fact that God meets us more than halfway when coming to us in Christ. Advent is a time when we learn afresh how to live with the tensions and the apparent ambiguities of this threefold coming of Christ—with the *then*, the *now*, and the *not-yet*.

What ought Advent to mean to us? This for sure: A heart and mind receptive to God; a willingness to be used by God; a humility asking to be a medium through which God speaks and works.

We do scant tribute when we read scripture for times and signs when Christ will fulfill His promise to come again. The time remains "top secret" with God. We are kept in suspense that we be kept alert. The coming is possible any day, impossible no day. We know what Jesus did for us at His first coming. With eager longing, we can live in anticipation of His coming again.

Prayer: Come, Lord Jesus, into my heart right now. Amen.

THOUGHT FOR THE DAY
Are we ready and alert for the coming of Jesus?
~John Birkbeck (Aberdeen, Scotland)

9

DO YOU LOVE JESUS?
Read Luke 18:15-17

Jesus said, "Verily I say unto you, Whosoever shall not receive the kingdom of God as a little child in no wise enter therein."
—Luke 18:17 (KJV)

It was the height of the Christmas season, and the large department store was crowded with shoppers.

My concentration on how much wrapping paper I should buy was abruptly broken when I heard a child's voice shout exuberantly, "I love Jesus! I love Jesus!" I turned around to see a little girl happily prancing along beside a middle-aged woman. A stunned silence fell over the store as the other shoppers looked at her. The woman, a little embarrassed by the child's enthusiastic outburst, leaned down and gently reproached her. The child stopped, gazed up at her with a perplexed look, and then stated emphatically and sincerely, "But I DO love Jesus! I really DO!"

"Well, that's good," the woman replied as they went on.

The event lasted only a few moments, and then the hustle and bustle began again. Yet that child taught me an important lesson.

Every Christmas—no, every day—all of us need to interrupt the busyness of our lives and ask ourselves if we can say truthfully, "I love You, Jesus! I really do!"

Prayer: Dear Lord, help us to never become so busy with the concerns of life that we forget about You. Amen.

THOUGHT FOR THE DAY
How do I express my love for Jesus?
~Debra Hemmer (California)

10 WAITING

Read Psalm 27:7-14

I wait for the Lord, my soul waits, and in his word I hope.
—Psalm 130:5 (RSV)

IT WAS CHRISTMAS EVE. The church was filled with expectant worshipers, but just below my balcony seat stood two special couples singing side by side—and waiting. Bill and Esther were waiting for death to claim Bill's terminally ill mother. Craig and Lynn were waiting for the birth of their first child.

How many others here are waiting for death or for life? I wondered. *How many are watching for the coming of God into joyful and tangled or pain-filled existence?*

Perhaps we are all waiting. I thought. *We are all in this church waiting and hoping for something.*

That is what Advent is all about, isn't it? Advent recalls Israel's centuries of waiting for the Messiah. The scripture reminds us that we, too, are waiting for God to move in our lives and in our world. Then Advent quietly insists that there *is* something worth waiting for. It tells us that our hope is not hollow, that as surely as God came to those people in the stable in Bethlehem, so God will come to us. With this assurance we can wait together, trusting and hoping in God.

Prayer: O God, we are waiting for Your action in our lives. We hope in You, trusting the witness of Him who has come, who comes, and who will come again. Amen.

THOUGHT FOR THE DAY
In hope and trust I will wait for God.

~Barbara P. Ferguson (Illinois)

HOPING

11   PROMISE OF SPRING
Read John 20:24-29

To have faith is to be sure of the things we hope for, to be certain of the things we cannot see.
—Hebrews 11:1 (TEV)

ON THE SUNDAY AFTER EASTER, the sun was shining beautifully. Our first hymn of the morning was "Thank God for the Promise of Spring" by W. J. Gaither (1973). With the sun shining through the windows and open door, the promise of spring, of renewal in Jesus Christ the risen Lord, was easy to believe that day.

But as pastor, I decided that the next time we sang that hymn would be on a dark, cold Sunday in the middle of winter. Then we would be affirming the coming of spring, even though the dullness of winter would seem to disprove the promise.

Our spiritual spring is a wonderful promise of God. We do not have to wait until physical evidence of it is before us to draw on the strength and renewal it offers. Our Lord says that new life and freedom from the burden of sin are ours now.

Prayer: Lord, we thank You for the beauty of all Your creation. Keep us determined to look beyond what we see, to embrace the eternal beauty of the Risen Christ, who gives us the promise of renewal and love forever. Amen.

THOUGHT FOR THE DAY
In the darkness of winter, God gives us the promise of spring.

~James A. Killian (Pennsylvania)

12 PRAISING GOD
Read Isaiah 61:1-9

The LORD has anointed me . . . to comfort all who mourn; . . . to give them a garland instead of ashes, the oil of gladness instead of mourning, the mantle of praise instead of a faint spirit.
—Isaiah 61:1, 3 (RSV)

SINCE MY TEEN YEARS, I have battled depression. Even after I became a Christian and learned the importance of forgiveness and keeping healthy relationships, that dark, ugly cloud found a way to park itself over my head. Getting up in the morning, doing my work, and taking an interest in life became more and more difficult.

I read a few years ago about a woman who also suffered from depression. She kept a praise diary, and when she felt depressed, she reviewed its entries. Her notes helped her realize she had much to be thankful for.

Following her example, I started writing a few lines of praise each day. Sometimes I was thankful for my husband and children. Other entries told of joy because of a special event that had happened. I even learned how to offer sacrificial praise to God for things in my life that scared or upset me, and to trust that God was in control.

Still today when I begin to feel low, I read my diary. Together, the entries weave a golden thread of God's love and presence in my life.

Prayer: Dear God, help me to praise You every day, regardless of how I feel. Amen.

THOUGHT FOR THE DAY
Even when we are hurt or angry, there is something to be thankful for.

~Annette Dunlap (North Carolina)

13   A Prism for God's Light
Read 2 Corinthians 3:18–4:6

God, who said, "Light shall shine out of darkness," is the One who has shone in our hearts to give the light of the knowledge of the glory of God in the face of Christ.

—2 Corinthians 4:6 (NASB)

Some rainbows dancing around the room fascinated me. They were made by light reflected through a prism hanging in the window. I became captivated by the rainbows and the sheer beauty of the prism itself. I had never seen the beauty of a prism before, and I thanked God for the beauty and for the rainbows.

In my quiet time the next day, the Lord helped me to see *myself* as a prism: God's light reflects through me. I am many-faceted; but sometimes the reflection of God's love is blocked by worry, distrust, unforgiveness, selfishness, and ingratitude.

A prism reflects only the light that goes through it. As I allow God to be in charge of my life, God uses me to shine love to others. I am only an instrument, but I can reflect God's love.

Prayer: God of light, shine through me so that those around me may feel Your holy presence in their lives. Amen.

Thought for the Day
God's light and glory are reflected in each of us.

~Miriam Kaylor (Louisiana)

14   MELTING SNOW
Read Psalm 8

The heavens are telling the glory of God; and the firmament proclaims his handiwork.

—Psalm 19:1 (NRSV)

MY HUSBAND AND I were experiencing painful estrangement from one of our adult children. One night, unable to sleep, I arose and looked out at the night sky. Light from a half-moon was shining, and shadows of the evergreen trees created a pattern on the drifted snow. I felt God's presence as I surveyed the tranquil scene.

I remembered how many other grieving and heartsick individuals through the ages have found comfort and purpose as the beauties of creation spoke to them of God's greatness and majesty. Gradually, as I stood there, new strength entered my heart and I felt new hope for our relationship with our child.

Prayer: God of all creation, we praise You. We thank You for Your love and for Your care for us all the days of our lives. We trust that You are working out Your purposes for us even in difficult times. In the name of Jesus, who taught us to pray, "Our Father in heaven, hallowed be your Name, your kingdom come, your will be done, on earth as in heaven. Give us today our daily bread. Forgive us our sins as we forgive those who sin against us. Save us from the time of trial, and deliver us from evil. For the kingdom, the power, and the glory are yours, now and for ever. Amen."*

THOUGHT FOR THE DAY
God speaks to us in creation.

~Hilda Bergen (Alberta, Canada)

---

*From *Prayers We Have in Common* © 1970, 1971, and 1975, International Consultation on English Texts.

15 LAMPLIGHT
Read 1 John 1:5-10

Thy word is a lamp to my feet and a light to my path.
—Psalm 119:105 (RSV)

ONCE WHEN I HIT AN ARID TIME in my writing, I began lighting a candle on my desk each day to remind me of God's presence as I worked. The candle didn't magically make everything better, but it did help me remember God was with me.

Then the dry spell lifted. My work excited me, ideas flowed freely, and several pieces held promise. While writing one morning, I glanced up. I had forgotten to light the candle!

How often this happens! When times are hard, I cry out for God's comforting presence. When times are good, I forget God's presence. I automatically switch on the lamp as I enter my dark apartment so I won't stumble. But when my life is going well and darkness seems far away, I often neglect my "faith lamp," forgetting that God illumines my way in good times as well as in bad.

Now each day I light that candle in hope and in celebration of God's presence. There will probably be days when I forget to light it, but even my forgetfulness will remind me that God's presence is steady. God is with me both in darkness and in light.

Prayer: God of light, help us to seek Your presence each day. Illumine our lives with graciousness and love. Amen.

THOUGHT FOR THE DAY
In good times and in bad, God lights our way.
~Jean M. Blomquist (California)

16 HELP AGAINST OUR INVADERS
Read Psalm 64

*With him is an arm of flesh; but with us is the LORD our God,
to help us and to fight our battles.*
—2 Chronicles 32:8 (RSV)

EARLY ONE MORNING I opened by Bible for my daily meditation and read about the invasion of Judah by Sennacherib, king of Assyria, and the resulting destruction of his army. The story fascinated me because I saw that an invisible and irresistible power had stopped the invader's arrogance. This power brought justice in response to the invocations and prayers of those who called upon God for help and freedom.

Today, in this time of false well-being and shallow abundance, many are distracted from their duties and deceived into following paths of self-indulgence and self-centeredness. Destruction of relationships, neglected children, and broken hearts are only a few of the results of this.

But the Holy Spirit will respond to our requests for help against our invaders—whatever or whoever these might be—as God responded to the requests of the people of Judah.

Prayer: Gracious Lord, free us from feelings of false righteousness. May we understand and fulfill our duties and let Your sublime peace fill us. In the name of Jesus. Amen.

THOUGHT FOR THE DAY
How am I seeking God's help against my invaders?
~Angiolina Montaldo (Turin, Italy)

17 GOD'S LIGHT
Read Habakkuk 3:17-19

Though the fig tree do not blossom, nor fruit be on the vines . . . the flock be cut off from the fold and there be no herd in the stalls, yet I will rejoice in the LORD, I will joy in the God of my salvation.

—Habakkuk 3:17-18 (RSV)

WHILE IT IS NECESSARY TO READ the Bible systematically to live fully by its teaching, there are times when an isolated verse can help us in a sudden need.

During World War II my husband was conscripted into the Royal Air Force. The day came when he had to leave me and our four children. In the darkness of early morning I said good-bye to him and listened to the fading sound of his footsteps along the deserted road. My world was shattered, and I was surprised when I heard the rattle of the milkman's van as if nothing had changed.

Desperately I prayed for courage and a word from the Bible I held in my hand. It fell open at the Book of Habakkuk, chapter 3. When I reached verse 17, it was as if a light had been switched on. I knew God was there with me. I felt as if all things in the verse had actually happened to me. "Yet I will rejoice," I read. It wouldn't be easy but, yes, I would try to do just that.

On many dark days since then, this verse has encouraged me to press on until once more I reach God's "high places."

Prayer: Thank You, God, for the light of Your words that guide us in the darkness. Amen.

THOUGHT FOR THE DAY
Look back and remember; look forward and trust.

~Kellsye M. Finnie (England)

18 THE LORD IS GOOD
Read Nahum 1:3-8

The LORD is good, a stronghold in a day of trouble.
—Nahum 1:7 (NRSV)

TWO OF MY THREE CHILDREN were sick; the right rear tire was flat; my dental crown was going to cost $300.00; I learned my retirement annuity earned only 4% interest last year. I was having a bad day.

Stuck in a rut of pessimism by these small things, I thought about all of the really bad things that are going on in the world: suffering, starvation, wars, hatred. Is God really not all that good?

Then I remembered my devotional from this morning: "The Lord is good." I needed that. I felt ashamed—but encouraged. The Lord *is* good. Like Peter looking at the waves, I had taken my eyes off Christ.

I learned something from my bad day: I may be faced with troubles beyond my ability to reconcile with God's goodness, but the essence of faith is trusting God when God's goodness is not obvious.

Prayer: Good Lord, we thank You that Your goodness is behind all that takes place in our lives. Help our unbelief. For Jesus' sake. Amen.

THOUGHT FOR THE DAY
No matter what trouble I face, I can always trust God's goodness.

~E. Langston Haygood (Alabama)

19   THE GIFT OF NEW LIFE
Read Psalm 130

I wait for the LORD, my soul waits, and in his word I hope.
—Psalm 130:5 (NRSV)

WITH ITS REMINDER TO WAIT IN HOPE, this psalm is appropriate for the season of Advent. Like the psalmist, we too have often waited for God to act and nothing seemed to happen. We pray for a sick child, an unemployed parent, a teenager on drugs, a marriage. We have faith that God will act, but the waiting is frustrating. The psalmist writes of waiting like the guard during the last watch of the night, like the one who longs for sunrise and the freedom to go home to bed. The hours seem long.

We are an impatient society. We want instant gratification and solutions to problems. We do not understand why God does not eradicate evil now. Yet we must wait.

In the Bible, we often see people waiting. The Hebrew slaves in Egypt waited for centuries for a liberator. The Hebrew people waited an entire generation to enter the promised land. Exiles from Judah waited for decades to return home. People waited for a Messiah. Early Christians waited expectantly for the kingdom of God.

We wait for God's time, but we wait in the hope that "with the Lord there is steadfast love, and . . . great power to redeem." Believing this helps us to wait with patience.

Prayer: O God, give us patience and trust in Your wisdom. Forgive our restlessness and grant us grace to know that You are working to bring what is best for us. Amen.

THOUGHT FOR THE DAY
While we wait, we can deepen our trust in God.
~William O. Paulsell (Kentucky)

20   Christmas Light
Read Matthew 5:13-16

The people that walked in darkness have seen a great light.
—Isaiah 9:2 (KJV)

I ARRIVED AT CHURCH to prepare for the Christmas Eve service to find that a power failure had left us with no lights. Groping my way to the office, I was able to find a single candle. As I sat in its feeble glow, about to give up hope of having a service that night, someone entered the darkened church. Soon another came, then another, until a congregation had slowly gathered. Now the light from my little candle seemed even more inadequate, as the faceless forms sat in the shadows.

After a short time of silence, a figure came quietly out of the dark, followed by others. As they approached, I could see that they were holding candles of their own.

They lit their candles from the one in my hand and returned to their places. We soon had a blaze of cheery light illuminating the entire church.

This is Christmas light: One small light, igniting others, until the world knows that the darkness can no longer prevail.

Prayer: Give us courage, dear God, to let the light of our faith shine where it is needed most by others. In Jesus' name. Amen.

THOUGHT FOR THE DAY
Because of Christmas, darkness can no longer prevail.

~William H. Doan (Kentucky)

LOVING

21 INTERRUPTIONS
Read Luke 2:15-20

Unto you is born this day in the city of David a Saviour, which is Christ the Lord.

—Luke 2:11 (KJV)

IT WAS THE BUSY, PRE-CHRISTMAS TIME of the year. This particular evening I had made plans to relax at home with my family. It would be the perfect way to unwind from the stresses of the season and absorb some real Christmas spirit.

The phone rang and the caller invited us to join a group of carolers to visit shut-ins. My family was enthusiastic. "But this would interrupt our plans for the evening," I said. Outvoted, I reluctantly agreed to forfeit my peaceful evening. As we traveled from house to house, it became apparent that we were sharing the true spirit of Christmas with many people. What had started out as an upsetting interruption was now bringing happiness to all involved.

As we sang the familiar carols, I reflected on that first Christmas when the shepherds were interrupted in their ordinary tasks by an angel and the Magi were interrupted in their study of the heavens by that bright new star. Think what they would have missed had they not been open to God's signs! Think what we miss when we refuse to allow God to interrupt our lives!

Prayer: Lord, help us to prepare for Your coming as we share the Christmas message with others. Amen.

THOUGHT FOR THE DAY
Let us be open to God's interruptions.

~John P. Jones (Maryland)

22 LOVE PAPERS
Read Philippians 4:2-8

Show a gentle attitude toward everyone. The Lord is coming soon.
—Philippians 4:5 (TEV)

MUCH OF THE WORRY AND ANXIETY we experience in our lives is the result of troubled relationships with those closest to us. Sometimes we reach an impasse in these relationships and find ourselves frustrated, not knowing how to move forward. One exercise that has helped me over the years is making a "love paper." On a piece of paper I write the name of the person I'm having difficulty with at the time. Then I proceed to list as many of his or her good qualities as I can. After I've finished, I pray a short prayer of blessing for this person and ask for willingness on my part to resolve the conflict and be reconciled.

As I reflect on the goodness in the other person, peace of mind gradually returns and I am able to relate with a kinder and more loving attitude. Many times this exercise is all that is needed to restore peace and open the lines of communication again.

Is there a relationship in your life that could be improved by making a love paper?

Prayer: Dear Lord, we thank You for our loved ones. We pray that You will bless, protect, and multiply Your goodness in them. Help us always to see that goodness. Amen.

THOUGHT FOR THE DAY
Always dwell on the fine, good things in others.
~Cathy Miller (Iowa)

23 A Gift for Us
Read John 4:5-14

Come, whoever is thirsty; accept the water of life as a gift, whoever wants it.

—Revelation 22:17 (TEV)

ONE ICY MORNING I WATCHED my grandfather put a pail under the spout of the iron pump in the farmyard. But when he lifted the handle of the pump, working it up and down, no water came bubbling from the spout.

"It needs priming," Grandfather said.

He went into the house for a dipper of warm water. Carefully he poured it into the pump, once more working the handle. As the warm water drained into the pump, Grandfather continued his patient pumping. At last we heard the welcome gurgle of water pouring from the spout in answer to Grandfather's persistent efforts.

Sometimes, like that iron pump, we are unresponsive—our lives are spiritually frozen. But God doesn't mean for us to endure a barren, unproductive spiritual life. God gave Jesus Christ so that we could have an abundant, joyful life. God is waiting to pour love into us, to prime the pumps of our lives, to make that love flow freely, bountifully through us. It is up to us, though, to keep the pumps working persistently, that God's love can flow through us to others.

Prayer: God of love, bless us with Your presence. Rouse us, refresh us, that we may share Your love with others. Amen.

THOUGHT FOR THE DAY
The water of life is offered freely to all.

~Dorothy Enke (Nebraska)

24 MAY I TOUCH YOU?
Read Ephesians 4:1-16

Accept one another, then, for the glory of God, as Christ has accepted you.

—Romans 15:7 (TEV)

I HAVE MANY SATISFYING EXPERIENCES as a volunteer at our church's evening center for persons who have handicapping conditions. One night I heard Kyle, a teenager who has a warm interest in others, talking with eleven-year-old Jenny. Jenny commented about getting her braces into the correct position. Kyle, who is blind, said, "Oh, I didn't know you wore braces. What kind do you have?"

"They are leg braces," she answered.

Tenderly Kyle asked, "May I touch your braces?" When Jenny said yes, he felt up and down the braces on her legs. "They must be very heavy," he said in a caring way. Kyle accepted Jenny as she was and enjoyed her as a person. He offered no pity.

How often do you and I try to build a meaningful relationship with a person who has a heavy burden or who is hurting in some way? Do we accept others naturally, as Kyle did, and express Christlike love? Or do we avoid persons who look different or who talk or think differently than we? At times we will need to say, "It must be very heavy," or "That must really hurt." Those are good thoughts. Such caring is Christian love alive.

Prayer: O Lord, help us to lovingly accept and reach out to those who have heaviness in their lives. In the spirit of Jesus. Amen.

THOUGHT FOR THE DAY
God wants us to show Christlike caring today.
~Charlotte Adelsperger (Kansas)

25   Heart for God
Read Psalm 42:1-11

Why are you in despair, O my soul? And why have you become disturbed within me? Hope in God, for I shall yet praise Him, The help of my countenance, and my God.

—Psalm 42:11 (NASB)

WHERE DID I LEAVE my sense of well-being? I had it only yesterday. Today, it is gone.

Is it beneath the piles of toys the children scattered through the house? Is it sandwiched between the layers of spills and crumbs that have accumulated in the kitchen? Did it fly out the door as we sped from one errand to the next? Where did it go? Of all the things I have lost—shoes, keys, books, best friends—the sense of quiet confidence is the one thing I can least afford to live without.

All the things and people in my life, and even my noblest intentions and dreams, are not enough. They fill my days but not the ache in my heart for God.

I am like a small child who wandered off, entranced by the colorful distractions of a crowded and cluttered store, calling now for God. God will not disappoint me. Because I know God loves me and will not leave me comfortless, I will wait for God's embrace.

Prayer: Lord Jesus, help me to walk faithfully by what I know and believe, not by unreliable feelings. Amen.

THOUGHT FOR THE DAY
God's love never wavers.

~Connie Walsh Brown (Maryland)

26 REAL TREASURES
Read Matthew 6:19-34

Where your treasure is, there will your heart be also.
—Matthew 6:21 (KJV)

WHEN MY SON WAS THREE years old, he would daily bring home a gift to me, something he had found on the dayschool playground. Some days it was a crumpled leaf; on other days it was the foil wrapping from a piece of chewing gum, a broken button, or a piece of shoelace. I tried always to be properly appreciative of these treasures.

One day he jumped in the car, obviously excited, exclaiming, "Mom, wait till you see the neat rock I found for you today!" He took from his pocket a rather angular, white, inch-size rock.

Trying to echo his excitement, I answered him in false amazement, "Oh, Will, you found me a diamond! It's lovely."

My son brought the rock up closer for me to view and said, "It's not a diamond, Mom. It's a really neat rock."

It occurred to me that my son had just given me a great gift. He had told me to see the ordinary, the everyday, and to appreciate it for what it is. God, who made everything good, meant for us to find pleasure in the common, not only the costly.

Prayer: Dear Lord, open my eyes to appreciate the wonder of the ordinary. Help me relish all the common creations You have made for me to enjoy. Amen.

THOUGHT FOR THE DAY

Every common rock can remind us of God's goodness.

~Jan Bailey McCauley (Texas)

27 KNOWING EACH OTHER
Read Matthew 18:1-4

He called a child, whom he put among them. . . .
—Matthew 18:2 (NRSV)

THE TRIP TO SEE MY GRANDMOTHER had been physically exhausting and emotionally difficult. Following a series of strokes and hospitalizations, Grandnanny was now in a nursing home. She did not know who we were. Her question to me, "And what kind of work do you do?" evoked poignant memories of her happiness at my ordination.

Within 24 hours of our return home, my mother called to say that Grandnanny had suffered another stroke. As my wife and two children and I sat at the kitchen table, we discussed whether to make a return trip. Exhausted, I observed, "I don't know what help it would be. She has no idea who we are." Eight-year-old Jennifer quickly responded, "But we know who she is, don't we, Daddy?"

We left the next morning.

Prayer: Thank You, God, for placing among us those who can vividly remind us to honor our fathers and our mothers as You have instructed us to. Amen.

THOUGHT FOR THE DAY
Family means remembering and caring for one another.

~Gary Brock (Tennessee)

28 THE LONELY ANGEL FISH
Read Acts 2:40-47

All the believers were together and had all things in common.
—Acts 2:44 (NRSV)

AMONG THE TWENTY TROPICAL FISH my grandson received for Christmas were two angel fish. He had not had these fish many days when one of the pair died, leaving the other one alone.

For days we watched the remaining angel fish. It seemed to be sick and sluggish, and it retreated into one corner of the tank. We thought the fish was lonely, so we concluded that we should purchase a few more angel fish to keep it company.

So we bought two new fish and added them to the tank. As soon as the first angel fish saw the new ones, it swam straight toward them, became lively, and swam around in company with them.

This fish reminded me that we cannot live our Christian lives in isolation. We cannot be solitary Christians. We need fellowship with other believers to help us grow in grace. Regular worship and fellowship reaffirm and strengthen our love for God and our faith and commitment to God's service.

Prayer: Eternal God, we praise You for the beauty of Christian fellowship and worship. In Jesus' name. Amen.

THOUGHT FOR THE DAY
A solitary Christian is like a fish out of water.
~Elaine S. Massey (Johannesburg, South Africa)

29 A STRANGER IN THE HOUSE
Read Ephesians 2:19-22

You also are built together spiritually into a dwelling place for God.

—Ephesians 2:22 (NRSV)

I STUMBLED DOWN the dimly lit hallway. Bleary-eyed, I opened the door to the sound of my daughter, Elizabeth Anne, crying. This precious infant is totally dependent on her mother and me. Yet despite her need, she is a stranger in our house. I hope and pray that over time we will come together as a family, friends, and fellow Christians. But for now, we are only beginning to know one another.

It also takes time to get to know God. If we do not spend time with God through prayer, Bible study, and worship, we can remain strangers even though we spend time in God's house. We are God's children, and that relationship brings obligations, just as being a part of a human family brings responsibilities and duties if we are to grow in our relationships.

Advent allows us the opportunity to come home again. I was baptized, confirmed, and married in the church. I have participated in all aspects of worship. However, over time apathy and unwillingness to serve have made me a stranger in my own church. This Christmas I am coming home to the church of my childhood and, most importantly, home to my Lord and Savior Jesus Christ.

Prayer: Lord Jesus, we welcome You to our homes, and most importantly, to our lives today. Help us not to be strangers in Your house. Amen.

THOUGHT FOR THE DAY
Christmas is a perfect time to come home to God.

~Louis A. Schopfer, Jr. (New Jersey)

30 LIGHT IN THE NIGHT
Read Isaiah 60:1-3, 19-20

Arise, shine; for your light has come, and the glory of the LORD has risen upon you.
—Isaiah 60:1 (RSV)

IN SWITZERLAND, IT IS CUSTOMARY to set up "Christmas trees for everyone" during the Advent season. In the darkest month of the year, the electric candles on these trees radiate light and warm our hearts with the glowing hope and expectation of Christmas, the birthday of our Lord and Savior.

It often surprises me to see Christmas trees suspended in the middle of the sky. These are fixed on the top of huge cranes at building sites. Their lights can be seen miles away.

Your life and mine may not be as spectacular as these Christmas trees in the sky. But Jesus Christ has called us to be lights for the world. The apostle Paul in his letter to the Philippians also compares the children of God to shining lights. (Some Bible translations use the words *torches* or *stars*.)

If we surrender ourselves to the Lord, He will empower us to radiate love to a world lost in the darkness of suffering and despair.

Prayer: Dear Lord Jesus, may the light of Your love shine through my life and bring others to You, to find healing and salvation. Amen.

THOUGHT FOR THE DAY
I, too, may become a candle or a star, burning for Jesus, the light of the world.

~Clara E. Csia (Zurich, Switzerland)

PREPARING

31 PREPARING FOR CHRIST
Read Isaiah 11:1-10 and Matthew 3:1-12

Prepare the way for the Lord.
—Matthew 3:3 (NIV)

DURING ADVENT WE FOCUS on preparing individually for the coming of Christ.

This motif of preparation is dramatized in one of the traditions of Mexico, *Las Posadas*. *Las Posadas* begins nine days before Christmas and symbolizes the time it took Mary and Joseph to travel from Nazareth to Bethlehem. For each of the nine days, the calling of Joseph and Mary at the inns of Bethlehem is reenacted.

The head of the household begins the ceremony by leading in prayer. Participants are divided into two groups, the pilgrims and the innkeepers. The pilgrims march through the house or neighborhood carrying lighted candles and singing a request for a room. At every inn they are refused. On Christmas Eve the pilgrims are welcomed at last. They enter, singing a joyful carol because they have found a place prepared for them.

Have distractions kept us from giving Christ the central place? During this Advent season, let us examine our hearts to find the places we have excluded Christ in our decisions, our work, our family life—and clear the way for His life to be lived through us.

Prayer: O Christ, be at home in my heart. Make me a dwelling place for Your love and grace. Amen.

THOUGHT FOR THE DAY
Have I made a place for Christ in my celebration?
~Mary Lou Redding (Tennessee)

32 THE LIGHT OF CHRIST
Read 2 Corinthians 4:5-6

Once you were darkness, but now in the Lord you are light.
Live as children of light.
—Ephesians 5:8 (NRSV)

"But, dear, chandeliers are so hard to clean!" someone said as I shared my delight at one of the treasures in the old house into which we were moving. We finally had a dining room, and a 75-year-old chandelier with crystal prisms hung proudly there.

After hearing those words, for months I dreaded cleaning that chandelier as it lit the room for our family dinners. Christmastime came, time to spruce up the house, time to do that dreaded cleaning of the light fixture.

What a joy as crystal after crystal, cleaned and shined, reflected light in a new way! Sparkling in the light, the chandelier was a thing of dazzling beauty. And the cleaning took only 30 minutes.

Cleaning the prisms made a great difference in the beauty of the dining room, yet it took little time from my life. I probably spent more time and energy dreading the task than in actually doing it.

It occurred to me that parts of my life might be shined up with just a little effort and not very much time. What simple little act might I do to reflect Christ more brightly? Perhaps extra time for praying, for writing a letter, for making a phone call, for doing a kind deed?

Prayer: God, take my life and shine through me with Your light of love. Let Christ be seen in what I do today. Amen.

THOUGHT FOR THE DAY
Let the light of Christ shine through you today.
~Robin Knowles Wallace (Wisconsin)

33 TIME FOR PRAYER
Read Matthew 6:25-34

God will bring you to judgment. So then, banish anxiety from your heart.

—Ecclesiastes 11:9-10 (NIV)

A YOUNG MAN WHO CAME to my medical clinic seemed anxious and in a great hurry. As I examined him, I asked him about his urgency. He told me that he had a hundred things to do and had to get back to work immediately. I advised him that if he continued at the same level of tension, he was sure to come back to me with high blood pressure.

After he left, I looked at my own busy life. As a doctor, I work from 9 A.M. to 10 P.M. Sometimes I worked round the clock. I spent so little time with my infant child that she did not recognize me when I went home. I asked myself, "Do I have the time to sit for even a few minutes and speak with God?" I realized that I tried to make my prayer time as short as possible to save time. With this kind of life, how can I hope to know God well?

We may feel that prayer is optional in our lives, and our busy schedules have encouraged us not to choose time for prayer. But it is a basic way that we come to know God and allow God to know us.

Prayer: Lord, help us to take time to thank You for giving us the whole day to carry on your work. Help us make time in our busy schedules for You. Amen.

THOUGHT FOR THE DAY
Do we make time for God?

~Leena S. Gole (Belgaum, India)

34 CHOICES
Read Joshua 24:14-17

Joshua said to the people of Israel, "Choose this day whom you will serve."

—Joshua 24:15 (RSV)

WHEN I THINK HOW DIFFICULT it is to make choices, I am reminded of a story about a young farm laborer. The employer showed appreciation for the laborer's hard work by giving him a light task—sorting potatoes. Finding the worker frantic a short time later, the employer asked what the trouble was. "It's not the work, sir," the youth replied. "It's these awful decisions."

Decisions are difficult, especially if they involve many minor details. No sooner is one trifling matter decided than another crops us, confusing us. This is one reason we should start not with the tiny individual bits and pieces but with underlying basics. These give reason for our choices in lesser matters. That is why Jesus said that we should seek first the reign of God and God's righteousness. Then, He said, the other things would be added.

Choosing Christ opens the way for us to see clearly the direction in which we should move. His life and teachings become a guide by which we can wisely make our decisions about issues great and small.

Prayer: O God, help us in making the one most important choice we will face in life: whom we will serve. Guide us in the path of right thinking and living day by day. Amen.

THOUGHT FOR THE DAY
Christ is our example in choosing God's way.

~Charles E. Fuller (Georgia)

35 Pass It On

Read Psalm 145:1-7

One generation will commend your works to another: they will tell of your mighty acts.

—Psalm 145:4 (NIV)

BELIEVING THAT ALL THINGS belonged first to the Lord, Mother joyfully utilized everything at hand to serve God. Growing up, I found her actions frustrating. Many times I vowed that in my house things would remain at home and not be always "down at church"!

I especially remember that Mother began early in each year collecting things she thought might be needed for the Christmas pageant. And on pageant night, my sister and I would marvel at how Mother had managed to fashion a jumble of materials from home into amazingly believable attire for Mary, Joseph, the Baby, and the rest. On that night we would be overjoyed that our modest belongings had contributed to making the occasion memorable.

That was long ago. Now I confess that when something is missing from my home, I don't worry. It nearly always turns up at church or wherever it was last needed. When I say this, my adult children chide that I am becoming "exactly like Grandmother"!

"Not quite yet," I say happily, "but I'm working on it!" I am glad to follow her example.

Prayer: Thank You, O God, for those whose enduring witness encourages us to follow You. Amen.

THOUGHT FOR THE DAY
How do I use what I have for God?

~Laura E. Cooper (Missouri)

36 A CHANGE OF FOCUS
Read Luke 18:1-8

If the Son sets you free, you will be free indeed.
                                        —John 8:36 (NIV)

ON A SATURDAY IN EARLY DECEMBER, my wife and I were very busy with housework. Our young daughters, Nyein and Htaw, said they wanted to do Christmas decorating. Since both my wife and I work during the week, the weekends are very busy and sometimes unpleasant. This weekend we felt we did not have time to do what our daughters asked, so we continued our housework. But our daughters did not give up. They asked us repeatedly to put up Christmas decorations.

Finally I dropped my work and persuaded my wife also to listen to our daughters' voices. We collected the things we had for Christmas decorating and began to do what we could at our small house. By the time we had finished, the atmosphere in our home had changed. Everyone was smiling and lighthearted, with bad tempers gone. Our daughters were jumping with joy.

Looking back, I realize that our focus had changed. Our world is full of business to take care of, duties, social activities, and housework. We often feel that the load is too heavy on us. But we were reminded on that December day that Christ our Savior wants to help us with our heavy load and fill us with joy.

Prayer: O Lord, teach us to come to You, and teach us to learn from one another. Amen.

THOUGHT FOR THE DAY
In this Christmas season and every day, the Lord wants to free us of our heavy burdens.

                                        ~Hla Tun (Yangon, Myanmar)

37

THE REAL STORY
Read John 1:1-5

A little child shall lead them.
—Isaiah 11:6 (RSV)

ONE DAY A FEW WEEKS before Christmas, I was reading a new book about the birth of Jesus to my 4-year-old son and his 3-year-old friend. My son soon became absorbed in the story, making comments that related events in the book to the nativity scene we had displayed on the fireplace. However, his little friend was easily distracted by the trappings of the "other" Christmas we had in the room—Santa Claus, reindeer, the Christmas tree, and especially the presents. She interrupted the story many times with questions that had nothing to do with Jesus.

When I thought about that experience later, I realized how often I am easily distracted by the trappings of this world—material possessions, success. I interrupt the telling of the real story many times. I need to learn to relate the events of God's story to my own life. Maybe then I can appreciate what the true meaning of Christmas is, today and every day.

Prayer: Thank You, dear God, for children who often show us Your way when we cannot find it for ourselves. Keep them always in Your loving care. Amen.

THOUGHT FOR THE DAY
This year I will be receptive to the real story of Christmas.

~Tricia Roe (Texas)

38 DECIDING OUR PRIORITIES
Read Ecclesiastes 3:1-11

Forgetting what lies behind . . . I press on.
  —Philippians 3:13-14 (RSV)

ONE thing is certain about a journey: You can't take everything you want with you.

My family was made painfully aware of this fact when we had to change our place of ministry after several years in the same location. In packing for our long journey, we had to decide what to leave and what, because of its essential or precious nature, we had to take with us.

Life is a journey. And on this journey sometimes we need to stop and examine our luggage in relation to our destination. If we are to develop as persons, we must eliminate negative attitudes, grudges and the memories of past failures. We must cultivate positive attitudes, cherished memories of past achievements, good habits, and helpful relationships.

As we come to the end of the year, this is a good time to think carefully about our priorities. How can we get rid of whatever hinders our social, moral, and spiritual development? How can we nurture those attitudes and virtues that will help us to be better persons? Let us press on to the mark of the high calling of Jesus Christ.

Prayer: Give us, O Lord, courage and resolution that we may eliminate evil not only in our lives, but wherever we meet it. Give us faith that we may cultivate the good in ourselves and in others. Amen.

THOUGHT FOR THE DAY

Using yesterday's experiences and tomorrow's hopes, I make the best use of today's opportunites.

~J. Emmette Weir (Nassau, Bahamas)

39 THE STARKNESS OF BETHLEHEM
Read Luke 2:1-7

She gave birth to her first son, wrapped him in cloths and laid him in a manger—there was no room for them to stay in the inn.

—Luke 2:7 (TEV)

PART OF MY WORK AS A PASTOR is to lead services at a local school. Before Christmas, one of the teachers telephoned me to ask if I would conduct a service. He spoke enthusiastically of how they had brightened up the stage "to make it look more Christmas-y."

Luke's Gospel portrays that first Christmas scene without bright lights, trees, holly, and tinsel. It was a dark, bare stable with only a manger for Jesus.

When I reflect on this, several questions come to my mind. Why do we try to escape from the starkness of Bethlehem? Is it because we are ashamed of the welcome the world gave to its Redeemer? Is it because we want to avoid the way of self-denial that Jesus lived and set as an example before us? Is it because we are afraid to face the challenge of Christmas to identify with the needs of the poor, the weak, and the helpless, as Jesus did?

I believe we can better understand the meaning of Jesus' birth when we look beyond the trappings of the Christmas celebration to the story of Christ in the Bible.

Prayer: Help me, God, to keep my eyes firmly fixed on Jesus so that I do not lose sight of the meaning of Christmas. Amen.

THOUGHT FOR THE DAY
How do I try to escape the starkness of Bethlehem?
~William H. McMillan (Erskine, Scotland)

40 DUSTY AND FADED
Read Romans 3:21-26

God so loved the world that he gave his one and only Son, that whoever believes in him shall not perish but have eternal life.
—John 3:16 (NIV)

LAST CHRISTMAS I RECEIVED a beautiful leaded-glass nativity of Mary, Joseph, and the infant Jesus. It sits on a small mirror base and is lighted from behind by a single, bright red candle.

When the holidays were over, I decided to leave the piece out to remind myself of Christmas and its true meaning. However, as the months passed, amidst the fragrance of spring flowers, the splash of kids in the pool, the brilliance of fall colors, I took it for granted. Not until December did I notice that a thick layer of dust had built up on the tiny mirror and that the candle had faded.

Had I done the same thing in my relationship with Christ? Was there dust on my commitment? Was my faith faded? Carefully I cleaned each piece of the glass until it shone in the winter sunlight. As I polished the smooth glass, I rededicated myself to the Lord and gave thanks for the gift of Christmas—a time when all of us can share in the birth of our Savior and the rebirth of our commitment.

Prayer: Dear God, as we again approach Christmas, let us see beyond the glittering tinsel to the steady light of Your gift to us: Our Savior, Jesus Christ. Amen.

THOUGHT FOR THE DAY
The spirit of Christmas can be with us all year if we remember Christ.

~Connie Winters (Ohio)

GOD
WITH US

 No Room
Read Luke 2:4-7

There was no room for them in the inn.
—Luke 2:7 (KJV)

THE RAIN BEAT ACROSS THE ROAD, whipping furiously around the bus shelter. Inside, a small knot of people huddled dejectedly into greatcoats and scarves. Only a few days remained before Christmas, and shopping had still to be done. A tired-looking woman struggled up clutching an overflowing shopping bag. A young child followed her. They tried unsuccessfully to squeeze into the shelter, out of the biting wind. The occupants near the entrance made no attempt to move closer together, although there was a large gap further along.

"I'm cold," whimpered the child. "Can't we go inside?"

"There's no room," replied the mother, wearily shifting her bag from one arm to the other.

The child looked up, her pinched face breaking into a smile, her treble voice penetrating clear above the noise of the traffic.

"It's just like the Christmas story, isn't it Mummy, when there was no room at the inn in Bethlehem, for Mary and Joseph and baby Jesus?"

There was a moment of stunned silence, then an uneasy shuffling inside the shelter. One or two persons smiled, as room was made for the mother and child.

Prayer: Lord, help us not to be selfish but to allow others to share our blessings. Amen.

THOUGHT FOR THE DAY
We can make room in our lives for those in need.
~Dorothy M. Loughran (England)

42 A PERPETUAL GUEST
Read John 14:15-21

Jesus said, "I will ask the Father, and he will give you another Helper, who will stay with you forever."

—John 14:16 (TEV)

SIX-YEAR-OLD MARTI raced through the kitchen door and plopped her Bible down on the counter. "Mom, may I set the table for dinner?" she asked breathlessly. I happily accepted her help but suggested she change her Sunday clothes first. "Mom, let me leave them on today, please!" she begged. I hesitantly consented.

Marti quickly gathered the plates, silver, and glasses, and arranged them neatly on the table. I had placed the food on the table, called her father, and sat down before I realized that Marti had set an extra place setting. "Marti, there are only three of us. Why did you set four places?"

She smiled broadly and replied, "Mom, we have a guest! My Sunday school teacher told us that when we are Christians, we always have Jesus with us. Our family is Christian, so Jesus is with us right now. I thought He might like to see me in my pretty dress and be with us at the table."

Marti's daddy and I smiled as we began our blessing, "Lord, thank You for always being with us. Help us to remember we can share every experience with You. Amen." "Amen," Marti echoed.

Prayer: Dear God, let us see You as through the eyes of children. Amen.

THOUGHT FOR THE DAY
The Holy Spirit is with us constantly.

~Nancy Keck (New York)

43 CHRIST HAS COME!
Read Jeremiah 31:31-34

The kingdom of God is not coming with things that can be observed; nor will they say, "Look, here it is!" or "There it is!" For, in fact, the kingdom of God is among you.
—Luke 17:20-21 (NRSV)

IN OUR COMMUNITY it is a custom to decorate at Christmas with mistletoe, a plant that grows high in trees. One holiday season my husband, Ronnie, and Uncle Allen set out to bring home plenty of mistletoe. We live in a rural area, and the task seemed simple. However, hours later, after searching and driving many miles, they came home with no mistletoe. When they drove into the driveway they both saw, at the same time, a huge bunch of mistletoe in a tree in our own yard. We have laughed about that adventure through the years, and we retell it every Christmas.

At times we are all like Ronnie and Uncle Allen when we look for Christ. We may go here and there, searching and wondering, then quietly realize that He is with us, here in our hearts and in the hearts of the people around us. That is something to smile about too. It is Christmas.

Prayer: Dear Jesus, thank You for giving us the freedom to celebrate life and the love and strength to bear each other's burdens. Thank You for coming into our hearts. Amen.

THOUGHT FOR THE DAY
Christ is near!
~Vickie Franks (North Carolina)

44 GOD AMONG US
Read Philippians 2:5-11

The Word became a human being and, full of grace and truth, lived among us.

—John 1:14 (TEV)

I TOOK A MISSION TEAM to an interior village in the state of Gujarat. As we reached the village square, many children and adults flocked around us. We talked to them of the love of God and of the sacrificial death of Jesus Christ. As we were returning, our six-year-old daughter, Alice, said, "Daddy, we must come and live with these poor people. If we do not live with them, how will they understand what we say?"

"Yes, it is very true," I answered. Unless we are willing to share the circumstances of the poor, how can we expect them to receive the gospel?

This is precisely what God did in the Incarnation. God became human and lived with us. Wherever we live, we can find many people who do not feel the reality of God's love for them. As the Word becomes flesh (see John 1:14) in our daily living, others will see God's love and care for them.

Prayer: O Lord of Incarnation, help us to show forth Your love, not only in our speaking but also in our daily living, loving, and caring. Amen.

THOUGHT FOR THE DAY
Today I will seek every opportunity to reveal that I am a messenger of Christ.

~K. V. Varkey (Kerala, India)

45

GOOD NEWS
Read Ezekiel 11:11-21

The angel said unto them, Fear not: for, behold, I bring you
good tidings of great joy, which shall be to all people.
—Luke 2:10 (KJV)

"BEHOLD, I BRING YOU good tidings of great joy." This was
the one sentence that Mark was to say at the Christmas
program. Everyone helped him rehearse it—his mother,
his father, his family, his director. He worked hard at
learning his line.

The evening came. The church was filled. Just before
he was to go on, he said the words to himself again. Step-
ping out, he saw the crowd of people. Silence fell on the
congregation as everyone waited for him to speak; but he
could not. The words had left him.

Raising his arms after a long pause, he said in a loud,
clear voice, "Boy, have I got good news for you!"

For two thousand years this good news has been
ringing in the hearts of Christians everywhere—good
news of a Savior who brings love, forgiveness, and ever-
lasting life to a world devoid of hope.

Let the bells ring, let the people sing, "Good news,
good news, good news!"

Prayer: Dear God, thank You for giving us the joy that
came with the birth of Jesus. Amen.

THOUGHT FOR THE DAY
Jesus' coming is the Good News.
~Pauline Kaufman (Ohio)

 LISTEN!
Read Matthew 13:1-9

He who has ears, let him hear.
    —Matthew 13:9 (RSV)

HAVE YOU EVER NOTICED when reading aloud with a congregation that the many voices at first seem jumbled? However, if we listen carefully, we can discern the leader's voice and can then capture the rhythm and read smoothly in unison.

Christmas can be very much like those first moments of congregational reading. At this time of year, we may be overwhelmed by the numerous voices that demand our attention. Our children and families make known their expectations. The marketing media would have us believe that it is blessed to buy. We are inundated by additional obligations and responsibilities. The seasonal exhortations become a cacophony. But wait! Can you hear it? Listen—it's a baby's cry! Tune out the clamor and hear the voice of the One for whom we celebrate the season. His joyful, plaintive appeal pierces the din, proclaiming that Christmas is the celebration of the gift of hope, given to a world sadly in need of that commodity.

Listen, that you may hear.
Listen.

Prayer: Thank You, Lord Jesus, for Your voice, which is ever present. Help us to listen more carefully, that we may hear what You have to say to us. Amen.

THOUGHT FOR THE DAY
Am I too busy to hear Christ's voice?
~Gioia Cattabriga (New Hampshire)

47 THE WONDER OF BIRTH
Read John 1:6-14

The Word became flesh and lived among us, and we have seen his glory, the glory as of a father's only son, full of grace and truth.
—John 1:14 (NRSV)

"THIS IS THE HAPPIEST MOMENT of life," I whispered as I gazed at our first baby daughter through the window of the humidicrib. Through weeks of hospitalization I had waited for this moment. A sense of the miracle of new life was indeed present and overwhelmed me. I had not understood until I experienced it personally.

For centuries before Christ's birth, Hebrew leaders and prophets had spoken of God's eternal care and compassion, the divine promise of deliverance. But how could humankind comprehend a loving, caring Omnipotence who is intimately involved in our human situation?

In the person of Jesus Christ, God became one of us, identified with all humanity, a loving friend, and the source of ultimate freedom. Jesus came to enable us to experience personally fellowship with the Eternal One.

Christmas is a time of celebration. Let us open our hearts and minds to experience once again the wonder of that moment in history when God became flesh and came to dwell among us.

Prayer: God Almighty, may Your truth enlighten our hearts and minds this Christmas. Grant us humble hearts to respond with love and adoration to the Christ Child. Amen.

THOUGHT FOR THE DAY
The birth of Christ opens up to us the wonder of who God is.

~Beryl Mortimer (Brisbane, Australia)

48   Something Is Happening
Read Isaiah 43:8-21

The LORD says, "Behold, I am doing a new thing."
                           —Isaiah 43:19 (RSV)

IN 1925, ON THE ANNIVERSARY of the birth of Abraham Lincoln, the *New York World* published a now-famous cartoon which pictured two Kentucky woodsmen. One woodsman asks, "Anything new happen lately?" The other responds, "Nothing much. Oh, there's a new baby over at Tom Lincoln's place."

Nothing much was happening—except the birth of a child who grew up to shape an entire country's concept of human rights and freedom.

There were probably folks in Bethlehem who said the same thing the night Jesus was born. "Anything new?" "Nothing much . . . a new baby born last night in a stable."

I wonder how often today we say that nothing much is happening, totally unaware of the new things which God wants to do in and through us. Maybe we are insensitive to the Christ who waits to be born in the ordinary, insignificant "stables" of our lives. Can we believe that God is ready to bring to birth something new in our own ordinary lives today?

Prayer: O God, I open the commonplaces of my life that they might become the birthplaces of Your new life for me in Jesus Christ. Amen.

THOUGHT FOR THE DAY
God wants to do something new in my life today.
                           ~James A. Harnish (Florida)

49 It's a Real Baby!
Read Matthew 1:18-25

When the time had fully come, God sent his Son, born of a woman, born under law.

—Galatians 4:4 (NIV)

THE SMALL MOUNTAIN CHURCH was crowded with parents and grandparents. Toddlers wandered in the aisles and around the platform. One of the preschool groups I teach was presenting a Christmas program, and the finale was the reenactment of the Christmas story. We were using one child's baby brother as Jesus.

As the angels appeared to the shepherds, one small angel lingered behind, near the manger which had been set up at the side of the platform. She was enthralled by the baby. As a toddler wandered up to the front of the church, the little angel said to her, "Look! It's a real baby!"

Though not performing her role as expected, she expressed by her words the idea of the Incarnation. God's Son came as a real baby—one just like us—to be born as we were, to experience what we experience, to show us how to live, and ultimately, to die for us. God knew this was the only way we could understand what our Creator is like. God became one of us!

Prayer: Dear God, thank You that You sent Your Son to experience the joys and hurts of life just as I do and to show me Your great love. Thank You for becoming one of us so we can become one with You. Amen.

THOUGHT FOR THE DAY
"Look! It's a real baby!"
~Shirley Crouse (Kentucky)

50 NEW LIFE
Read John 1:1-18

The Word became a human being and, full of grace and truth, lived among us.

—John 1:14 (TEV)

A SMALL BOY, LOOKING AT A PICTURE of his absent father, turned to his mother and said, "I wish Father could step out of the picture and be here with us."

That is what happened at Christmas! God stepped out of the heavenly picture and came to be with us as a human being—Jesus of Nazareth. Because of the Incarnation, we know what God is like and that God is with us.

The good news of Christmas—God with us—goes much deeper than colored lights, evergreen trees, stuffed stockings, and special foods. It is an invitation to new birth, a new beginning. "To all who received him, who believed in his name, he gave power to become children of God who were born, not of blood or of the will of the flesh or of the will of man, but of God" (John 1:12-13).

Christmas tells us that God has come to us, bringing us the good news that we all can have a new birth and that we forever belong to God.

Prayer: Gracious Father, we thank You for sending Your Son to us so that we can know what You are like. We thank You that You have come to dwell in us. Amen.

THOUGHT FOR THE DAY
Share the good news of Christmas.
~Esther McIlveen (British Columbia, Canada)

51 "O HOLY NIGHT"
Read Matthew 1:22-25

The shepherds said to one another, "Let's go to Bethlehem and see this thing that has happened."
—Luke 2:15 (TEV)

IT WAS A RAINY NIGHT—raining outside and raining in my soul. I was driving home from work two days before Christmas. "O Holy Night" came on the radio. Sunshine broke over my soul. God was there.

We humans move between agony and ecstasy in this life. The spiritual intrudes into the earthly. Sometimes we welcome this intrusion, as when it reassures us of God's presence and love. Sometimes it is not so welcome, as when God is seeking to lead us not where we wish to go but where we ought to go.

When we contemplate the sin, suffering, and tragedy in the world, we live on the edge of tears. But when we contemplate the Christmas message—God Incarnate, Emmanuel, God with us—our hearts beat with renewed hope and joy.

God is so much with us in the Christmas story that priorities are set right. Because of Christmas we can move from the agony of doubt and fear to the ecstasy of living in Christ.

Prayer: O Emmanuel, live in us as we prepare to greet You anew this Christmas. Renew our spirits with Your goodness, and thrill our hearts with Your joy. Amen.

THOUGHT FOR THE DAY
Christmas never fails those who listen for the angels.
~Hiram B. Holdridge (Illinois)

52 PEACE ON EARTH?
Read Isaiah 11:1-9

Glory to God in the highest heaven, and on earth peace among those whom he favors.

—Luke 2:14 (NRSV)

I REMEMBER VIVIDLY my first Christmas in Vietnam. It was 1970, and I was in a hot, tropical war zone. The Christmas season didn't seem much different to me than any other season. I spent most of the night before Christmas on guard duty. With a steel helmet on my head and an M-16 rifle cradled in my arm, the possibility for peace on earth seemed remote to me.

And yet I remember thinking in the early hours of Christmas morning that perhaps this was not so very different from the first Christmas. The night was probably as dark for the shepherds in the field as that night was for us in Vietnam. And it was on a night like this that Jesus came into a lost world with a ray of hope. So as dawn broke on Christmas morning, in my heart I could hear, however dimly, the song of the angels.

May the Prince of Peace be born anew in each of our hearts this Christmas season.

Prayer: Prince of Peace, we ask You for peace in the world and peace within us. Amen.

THOUGHT FOR THE DAY
Peace on earth begins within our hearts.

~Brian Detrick (Virginia)

53 AN UNHAPPY SHEPHERD
Read Luke 2:8-20

In that region there were shepherds out in the field, keeping watch over their flock by night. And an angel of the Lord appeared to them.

—Luke 2:8-9 (RSV)

ON THE LAST SUNDAY before Christmas in 1957, I made my stage debut in the Christmas play at my home church. As the youngest cast members and apparently too young to be trusted with learning and reciting lines, we first graders were shepherds.

I was unhappy. Why couldn't I be a wise man, colorfully dressed and bearing valuable treasure? Why not an angel? Or Joseph? Instead, it was my lot to wear dull clothes and have nothing interesting to say. Nobody chooses the shepherd's role in the Christmas play!

Back then, I did not understand that the shepherds on Luke's stage were also considered to be last and least. They were most unlikely recipients of the angelic message. And yet to them the announcement first comes. God considers no one untouchable, recognizes no class distinctions, and kicks over racial and ethnic barriers. The "good news of great joy" comes to all.

Prayer: Help us to be as free in sharing Your love as You are in giving it, O God, that we may know the fullest benefits of Your greatest gift in Christ our Lord. Amen.

THOUGHT FOR THE DAY
The person I esteem least is thoroughly beloved of God.

~Byron L. Rohrig (Indiana)

54   CHRIST IN CHRISTMAS
Read John 1:1-5

The Word became flesh and made his dwelling among us.
—John 1:14 (NIV)

TRY AS I MAY, the role of Christ in my Christmas tends to remain superficial from the lighting of the first candle on the Advent wreath to the closing hymn at midnight service. However, after Christmas Day—after the shopping, the wrapping, the decorating, the cooking and entertaining—Christ finally comes into my Christmas.

In that longed-for lull, when the refrigerator is still full of leftovers from Christmas dinner and the house is cleared of ribbons and wrappings, I finally sit quietly, during these days before Epiphany, in the pine-scented candlelight, and meditate on the meaning of Christmas.

I marvel once again at the unspeakable love of a Creator who gave us this bountiful earth, as well as lungs to breathe its air and eyes to see its beauty, but still was not satisfied until He had come to us cold and homeless as a helpless child.

To contemplate this awesome loveliness is almost more than one can bear. I know that if I were even to glimpse this brilliant love I, like Paul, would be left blinded, brokenhearted over the state of my soul.

Prayer: Light Eternal, illuminate our dark souls, drive away ignorance, prejudice, and superstition. Replace these stifling limitations to our spirit with a childlike wisdom and faith. In Christ's name. Amen.

THOUGHT FOR THE DAY
Consider the awesome love of God.
~Nickell Ceraldi (North Carolina)

55

JOY
Read Luke 2:15-20

Suddenly a great army of heaven's angels appeared with the angel, singing praises to God: "Glory to God in the highest heaven, and peace on earth to those with whom he is pleased!"
—Luke 2:13-14 (TEV)

HERE WE ARE, and here is the world. Everything seems to be changing, yet nothing has changed at all. There are wars and rumors of wars; the poor we always have with us. What is to be done?

We can complain. We can contort our faces into frowns and whine. We can howl in the darkness or pull in our hopes and snuggle together against the cold world. We can string a line of colored lights on an artificial tree and try to make merry. What can anybody do?

Little wonder that much of our life is spent in lamentation rather than celebration. It's Good Friday all over again. Crucifixion is always in the news—wars, refugees, sickness, political oppression, immorality, death. The gloom is overwhelming.

This December, like all others I can remember, there are crosses everywhere, and the news is little more encouraging than it was last year. So we gather in church to sing sad songs, catalogue our sins, wring our weak hands, crawl upon our knees, and beg for mercy. The world gets worse and so do we.

Then what's this? On the coldest of cold nights, among the most enslaved of all oppressed people, in the most insignificant of all backwater towns, it happens. A group of poor shepherds is startled by the flutter of wings. The valleys rumble, and the darkened heavens explode in signs and wonders. A young woman sings a song of victory, and a stable warms with the cry of a newborn.

Gradually, the news spreads. People grow restless, tyrants tremble, and Caesar's legions are alerted. A star leads even foreigners to Bethlehem. Angels sing before the once-silent poor, and prophets shout in the wilderness that the time is full. The child cries and the drama begins.

Once again we of little faith are wrenched from our despair. Once again we learn what we so easily forget: *God with us.* It has happened so often in our history, in our lives. Why must it always surprise us on Christmas Day? Let the whole world resound with the shout: God is with us, doing for us what we cannot do for ourselves. Everything has changed. Nothing is fixed or final now. Wedging into our tidy, dull little world, the Anointed One takes charge and leads us to freedom. In your life and mine, in the whole, hurting, sad old world, God is with us.

Hear that raucous chorus this day. Let your feet move to a new beat. Let cynicism give way to Good News. Today nothing is appropriate except joy. Come to Bethlehem; see the whole world turned upside down by the God who is pleased to be one of us, one with us, one for us.

Prayer: God of joy, quicken our hearts as we welcome the Christ Child once again. Amen.

THOUGHT FOR THE DAY

What difference does it make in your life that God is born in our world this day?

~William H. Willimon (North Carolina)

56 BORN IN OUR HEARTS
Read Luke 2:1-7

She gave birth to her first-born son.
—Luke 2:7 (RSV)

I HAD ALWAYS WONDERED what it would be like to go to Bethlehem. After all, it is the place where Jesus was born. I had thought, What a joy it would be to stand where God's love was born in human flesh!

I finally traveled there this year, and my life was truly blessed on that journey. Going to Bethlehem was all I had hoped it would be—and more. Going there has brought the scenes of the Bible vividly alive in my mind and heart. Going there has been an experience I will never forget.

Yet, since coming back, I have learned a strange truth. Namely, we don't have to go to Bethlehem to experience Bethlehem. Rather, Bethlehem has a mysterious way of coming to us. That is because Bethlehem is not merely a place on a map where the love of God was born. It is also a place in the human heart where love for God, others, and self can be born. And that divine love is born there each time we give food to the hungry, water to the thirsty, and clothing to the naked. Bethlehem is wherever God's giving love is born in human relationships.

Prayer: God of love, may the words and feeling of Christmas give birth to hope in our hearts this holy season. In the name of Your Son we pray. Amen.

THOUGHT FOR THE DAY
Jesus can be born in us every day.
~Paul Aiello, Jr. (Michigan)

57 THE GIFT OF SELF
Read John 10:7-10

In him was life, and the life was the light of all poeple.
—John 1:4 (NRSV)

SHE LIVED ALONE in a mobile home in an area of Miami that many people considered dangerous. She was about to celebrate her 99th Christmas.

A well-dressed man carrying a poinsettia arrived at her door on the afternoon before Christmas. With great caution she demanded to know who was there. She was surprised to discover that it was her doctor, for she was used to seeing him in a white coat. With a smile that brushed away most of her wrinkles, she invited him in for a chat and cup of coffee.

When I visited her the next day, she told me about the event of this special visitor with so beautiful a gift. With mellow, joyous restraint, she said, "Pastor, he didn't send the gift, he brought it himself!"

How well she expressed the Incarnation—God coming into our hearts and lives. And God's gift was very God! As John expressed it in his Gospel, this life brought light to everyone.

Prayer: Eternal Love, thank You for coming in person with life's greatest gift. Amen.

THOUGHT FOR THE DAY
God is willing to come to every heart in person.
~Lee R. VanSickle (Florida)

58 MORE THAN A MANGER
Read Matthew 18:1-6

Whoever becomes humble like this child is the greatest in the kingdom of heaven.

—Matthew 18:4 (NRSV)

I WAS SHOWING MY CHRISTMAS TREE trimmed with artificial Easter eggs to a friend and her 10-year-old son. While she was complimenting me on my cleverness for finding such an unusual use for the ribboned eggs, her son stood thoughtfully before the tree. When our glib chatter died down, the boy said, "It's all right to use Easter eggs on a Christmas tree. The baby in the manger is not all. There is also the cross and the resurrection."

I was amazed at the depth of the child's insight. In my zeal to create something beautiful (and be praised for it), I had missed the real reason we celebrate—the gift of eternal life.

Since then, when I get caught up in the whirl of gift giving and decorating, I pause to reflect on the true meaning of Christmas. In my mind's eye, I see again a small boy standing before a Christmas tree, and I hear again his words, "There is also the cross and the resurrection."

Prayer: Lord, help me see beyond the decorations of the season to the beauty of Your love for me. Amen.

THOUGHT FOR THE DAY
There is more to Christmas than a baby in a manger.

~Ollie A. Thorsell (Texas)

59   TRAVELING HOME
Read Luke 2:25-38

[Simeon] took [Jesus] up in his arms, and blessed God and said, Lord, now lettest thou thy servant depart in peace, according to thy word: For mine eyes have seen thy salvation.
—Luke 2:28-30 (KJV)

I REMEMBER A JOYFUL ADVENT season, preparing to celebrate the coming of Emmanuel. But three days before Christmas, the illness of our beloved grandmother caused a curtain of sadness to fall. Six days later she passed into the presence of her Lord.

In Gramma's church, we celebrated her life and homegoing with thanksgiving. But the pain of separation became overwhelming, and I found myself inwardly crying out, "Come back! Come back!"

At nightfall, the scattered families left the gathered circle to begin their long drive home. Christmas lights shone from the windows of all the little towns along the way. Suddenly, after a long stretch of lonely road, a glowing manger scene dissolved the wintry darkness in front of a country church. "Emmanuel, Emmanuel—God with us, God with us," somewhere deep inside me the music rang. In the midst of sorrow, God was there.

Gramma was home. But we were travelers still, bearing gifts, following a star.

Prayer: Lord, as we pass through the shadows of life, when all we have is emptiness, we bring just that, knowing You will fill us with joy and love again. Amen.

THOUGHT FOR THE DAY
Under the appearance of loss may lie great gain.
~Judy Imrie (Ontario, Canada)

60 CHRISTMAS BREAD
Read Luke 11:5-13

"For everyone who asks receives, and everyone who searches finds, and for everyone who knocks, the door will be opened."
—Luke 11:10 (NRSV)

LUCY and her sister Vilma were blind from birth. Their parents were poor, and their family faced many difficulties.

"When I was ten years old," recalls Lucy, "my father lost his job. It was during the Chrtistmas season, and we soon realized there would be no gifts. Christmas would seem just like any other day.

"On Christmas morning we were sitting at the breakfast table. Mother started praying the Lord's Prayer. When she came to the words *give us this day our daily bread*, her voice gave way; and I noticed that she was crying.

"My sister and I continued the prayer to the end. When we finished, someone was at our door. It was our neighbor who brought us fresh bread for our breakfast.

"It was only when I sensed the fragrance of fresh bread and the joy expressed by Mother that I discovered there had been no bread on our table.

"On that Christmas day, God had made Himself present in our home," says Lucy.

Prayer: O God, we can thank Thee even for difficulties. They are the cement that helps us build our spiritual lives. Amen.

THOUGHT FOR THE DAY
God answers prayer.
~Cláudia Sant' Anna (São Paulo, Brazil)

GOD
FOR US

61 CHRISTMAS IS GOD WITH US
Read Luke 2:1-7

[Mary] gave birth to her first-born son and wrapped him in swaddling cloths, and laid him in a manger, because there was no place for them in the inn.

—Luke 2:7 (RSV)

ALMOST TWO THOUSAND YEARS have passed, and still the story of the birth of Jesus proclaims the certainty that God is with us.

Every Christmas we celebrate Jesus' coming into the world by giving presents, having family reunions, attending special church services. Above all else, we reaffirm the giving of our life to Jesus—the only gift he desires from us.

I believe Jesus is happy with our demonstrations of love to Him and to the people with whom we live. I also believe that Jesus' greatest joy is to feel daily that our hearts belong to Him.

We are grateful for Jesus' coming into the world, for His ministry of love, for His sacrifice on the cross, for His resurrection. And we rejoice that He is with us, not just once a year but every day during all the years.

Prayer: Dear God, we thank You for the marvelous gift of Your Son. Teach us to love Him always. Amen.

THOUGHT FOR THE DAY

Christmas reminds us that we are to love God above all else.

~Edy Rosa Walter Capelao (Rio Grande do Sul, Brazil)

62 THE ETERNAL LIGHT
Read 1 John 1:1-7

God is light and in him there is no darkness at all.
—1 John 1:5 (NRSV)

I STRUGGLED INTO THE KITCHEN, juggling groceries, brief-case, and mail, and finally managed to hit the light switch with an elbow. No electricity! The first day back at work after Christmas had been tough enough, but now this!

I bumped my way through the house to find matches. Now, for the candles. In the dying rays cast by the setting sun, I saw the outline of my Advent wreath in the center of the living room. I had nearly packed it away the day before.

I lit the now-short outer candles and then the center Christ candle. I relaxed as I sat down. The glow of the candles lighted a cold, dark room and warmed my weary soul.

Those lights had been my beacon all during Advent and Christmas. Now they shone brightly to remind me that the light of Christ knows no single season.

I had no electricity, no heat, no water; but, in that moment, I had peace in the eternal Light.

Prayer: O Christ, illumine me with Your loving Spirit. Cast Your light into the dreary corners of life until my heart glows with the reflection of Your grace. Amen.

THOUGHT FOR THE DAY
The light of Christ shines through every night of the soul.

~Barbara W. Short (North Carolina)

63

THE FLIGHT INTO EGYPT
Read Matthew 2:10-18

Trust in the LORD, and do good; so shalt thou dwell in the land, and verily thou shalt be fed.
—Psalm 37:3 (KJV)

I HAD PASSED BY THE CHRISTMAS figurines in our shop often. Sitting on the shelf, unarranged, they held little meaning for me. Then one day when I was feeling a sense of loss because of many changes coming about in my family, my eyes rested upon a figure of Mary, Joseph, and the baby Jesus. Mary, seated on a donkey, sheltered the infant in her arms. Joseph turned his eyes toward heaven as he led the donkey.

Suddenly their flight into Egypt seemed to be a symbol of my life at that point. God led the holy family to a safe place to protect the young child Jesus and the ones to whom Jesus had been entrusted. God had prepared the way for the birth of Jesus and provided, through the gifts of the Magi, money for their journey and sustenance during the years in exile. And God scheduled the return trip as well.

My spirits rose as I realized that I did not have to be fearful because of my changing circumstances. Our God who provided for and protected the holy family long ago still does the same for us. Glory to God in the highest!

Prayer: Dear Lord of the universe and Protector of Your children, we thank You for Your steadfast love and kindness. Help us to remember that You are with us as we face daily pressures and hardships. Amen.

THOUGHT FOR THE DAY
God offers us courage and guidance in times of change.

~Mary E. Smith (Connecticut)

64 GOD'S PRESENCE
Read Genesis 28:10-15

Lo, I am with you alway.
—Matthew 28:20 (KJV)

SOON AFTER THE BIRTH of my second child, I felt the burden of days filled with the same routine—changing diapers, soothing hurt feelings, cooking dinners, and doing load after load of laundry. I hardly had time to breathe, much less set aside specific time just to be with the Lord. I was exhausted, and God seemed far away.

Where are You, God, when life turns into one ordinary day after another? I wondered.

One rainy morning I stared out the window, taking a few moments to myself before my sons awoke. I noticed a row of raindrops hanging from the window pane, each exactly like the one next to it. Clear. Round. Ordinary. As I watched, the sun came out from behind a cloud, lighting the gray morning and sending from one raindrop a brilliant rainbow of color. As I sat there, a small voice spoke in my heart: *Even ordinary things become beautiful if the light hits them in just the right way.*

In that moment I realized that even the smallest amount of time with the Lord could turn my day into something beautiful. As busy as I was, I knew that God would help me find that time.

Prayer: Lord, when my eyes become blind to Your wonders, help me see the rainbows You create each day. Amen.

THOUGHT FOR THE DAY

God has the power to make something beautiful out of the most ordinary situation.

~Teresa J. Cleary (Ohio)

65

THE LOVE OF MISSY
Read John 15:12-17

Let us love one another; for love is of God.
—1 John 4:7 (RSV)

LOOKING down at my dog, Missy, as she lay relaxed in sleep, I compared her to the trained dogs I had just read about. Missy has given much to our family in her life. She is not trained for anything special, but she can find a dog biscuit lost under the cupboard. She can hear a spoon touch a dish three rooms away and come running for a sample. She is not much as a watchdog, but she does have one important ingredient of life—love.

We got Missy as a puppy. She was always ready to run, jump, and play. She even does some tricks. Yet, when my wife was confined to bed with cancer, Missy lay at the foot of the bed ready to be company or just a quiet companion. She was always ready to share the warmth of her love.

Why does she love so much? Looking back over the years, I believe that I know why. She has never known anything but love from her family.

Why can't we also love and trust as deeply? God has poured His love upon us since creation. Perhaps, if we would open to God as Missy has to her family, we would find His love flowing in us and we, too, could share that love with the world.

Prayer: Our Father, help us to know Your love fully and to express it to those we meet each day. Amen.

THOUGHT FOR THE DAY
Trust God's love; share it with the world.
~Robert C. Cartwright (Maryland)

66 GOD'S ROCK POLISHING
Read Matthew 4:18-22

[Jesus] said to them, "Follow me, and I will make you fish for people."

—Matthew 4:19 (NRSV)

WHEN OUR SON WAS YOUNGER, his heart's desire for Christmas was a rock polisher. In preparation for the day he would have this prized possession, he spent weeks collecting rocks. There were rocks in pockets, rocks in the carpet, rocks in the washing machine. It was a relief finally to have them in the polisher.

I remember hearing the hum of the polisher in the garage, day after day. And when the rocks came out, their beauty was overwhelming. They shone with a colorful brilliance that one could never imagine could be hiding in a piece of rock picked up from a graveled street.

Jesus did not go into the temples, the courthouses, or any of the learned, upper-class establishments to pick his disciples. He went out to the seashore, to the laboring class, even to the despised and rejected people and said, "Follow me." And what did He do with these "rough stones"? He polished them. He refined them. We have but to read the Acts of the Apostles to see the results of Jesus' teaching, and the power of the Holy Spirit in these disciples' lives. Rough stones? The roughest. Can God likewise use us? We can be sure of it.

Prayer: Thank You, Lord, that You still use ordinary people to be Your disciples and share Your message. Amen.

THOUGHT FOR THE DAY

Even the roughest stones can become brilliant and beautiful in God's hands.

~Madeline Peterson (Nebraska)

67 WALKING WITH JESUS
Read Galatians 5:22-26

It is no longer I who live, but Christ who lives in me.
—Galatians 2:20 (RSV)

I WAS A CHURCH-GOING PERSON during my childhood and youth years, but I did not involve myself in church activities. I was a silent person in my high-school days.

During my fourth year in high school, I happened to attend the Christian Institute for youth. On the last day, I had a personal encounter with the Lord and received Christ as my personal Savior. This was my first step with Jesus, a step of total submission of my whole life.

Other steps followed. My Christian life was nurtured during college years. My guiding principle was "Seek God first." I involved myself in church and school activities. A major step was the affirmation of God's call for me to be a deaconess church worker. What are the next steps with Jesus in my life? Only God knows.

Without Jesus, life is meaningless. Have you taken the first step in your life with Jesus? Once we take that step, we can say to ourselves, "It is no longer I who live, but Christ who lives in me."

Prayer: Dear God, I receive Jesus as my Savior in my life. Help me to live the steps of my life with Jesus. In His name. Amen.

THOUGHT FOR THE DAY
The sure path in life is walking with Jesus.
~Esther P. Gabuyo (Luzon, Philippines)

68

LEGACY OF PEACE
Read John 14:25-31

Jesus said, "My peace I give to you; not as the world gives."
—John 14:27 (RSV)

THE "PEACE" THE WORLD GIVES is temporary. The peace which is merely the absence of war depends on circumstances and may be determined by who has the most weapon power. When such peace exists, it seldom endures for long and at times has to be enforced by armed troops. Some seek a kind of peace through drugs, alcohol, or escape of one kind or another. Others try meditation or relaxation exercises or withdraw to remote places in search of peace.

When praying for His followers, Jesus did not ask that they be taken from the world but that they might have strength to live in it. Jesus brings grace to forgive sin, reduce guilt, and find peace from within as we find ourselves in Him. The only peace the world gives is the temporary absence of stress or turmoil. The peace Christ gives is a presence, an addition, a filling. The Holy Spirit can actually use the world's stress and turmoil to break us, melt us, mold us, and fill us with "peace that passes all understanding."

Prayer: Dear God, thank You for the enduring peace that comes from within and is totally independent of circumstances. May we recognize that You are the only source of peace and relax our hearts and minds to receive Your gift. Amen.

THOUGHT FOR THE DAY
God offers lasting peace to the world and to us.
~Kathleen S. Lewis (Georgia)

69   COUNT YOUR BLESSINGS

Read Psalm 111

Great are the words of the LORD, studied by all who have delight in them.

—Psalm 111:2 (NRSV)

ONE DAY I WAS CLEANING my cupboard and throwing away old books. Among those books I found a birthday card sent to me four years earlier. In it had been written two Bible verses that said God's love and providence would always be given to me.

As I looked at the card, I found myself thinking about those verses of scripture. I looked back to the past and was surprised to realize how they have been fulfilled. God has indeed blessed me and my family. Over the past four years God has changed our lives. My parents accepted the Lord. We have been able to have a decent house to live in. The Lord has given me wisdom and strength to finish my studies.

I realize more and more how fortunate I am to be a child of God. And one way to be reminded of that fact is to count God's blessings—one by one.

Prayer: Thank You, Lord, for all Your blessings. We are grateful for Your love and providence that never fail us. Amen.

THOUGHT FOR THE DAY

We will always be surprised when we count God's blessings to us.

~Dyah Tobing (Indonesia)

70   TENDING BARREN STALKS
Read Hosea 14:4-8

If God so clothes the grass of the field, which is alive today and tomorrow is thrown into the oven, will he not much more clothe you?

—Matthew 6:30 (NRSV)

FROM EARLY SPRING TO LATE FALL, my husband, Bob, has a magnificent flower garden. He loves having people stop to admire his garden and will proudly give them a tour. The garden is for everyone to enjoy, a tribute to God who shows love for us through nature. It is as if Bob daily wraps his arms around his garden and offers the bouquet to God. What others do not see is that during the freezing months of winter, Bob lovingly tends barren stalks or shoots, nurturing and protecting them from wind and ice, seeing the potential for spring.

Seeing Bob in his garden in January reminds me of God's love and of how God tends us. Through the dismal winters of the spirit and through the everydayness of our lives, even when no blooms or fruitfulness seem near, God is at work. Through our Bible study and prayer, God tenderly readies us for the bursting forth of our spring. God gives us strengthened hands to join with other hands in service, renewed minds to help troubled minds, and singing hearts to give hope to those who have forgotten how to sing.

Prayer: Lord, thank You for caring about me and tending me so that I may produce the fruit of Your Spirit. Amen.

THOUGHT FOR THE DAY
God not only created us but tends us faithfully.

~Maxine Powell (Kentucky)

GOD THROUGH US

71 PUTTING AWAY THE BOWS
Read Philippians 2:1-11

You have fellowship with the Spirit, and you have kindness and compassion for one another.

—Philippians 2:1 (TEV)

THE FRANTIC LAST MINUTE RUSH is over. Bright, bow-bedecked packages have disappeared from under the tree, and a rainbow of crumpled paper spills out of a large cardboard carton.

Bows and curly ribbons, saved each year, have been carefully placed in a box. As I tape it closed, I begin thinking. These bows were used on presents that were bought and wrapped while our hearts were overflowing with the warm, loving spirit of giving, the Christmas spirit. No gift was too expensive or too hard to find if it would make someone we loved happy.

Now, I wonder, will we pack away that generous spirit along with the bows, to be brought out again next year? Tomorrow, will we forget the joy of today? Will we still be willing to help fill a food basket for a needy family, clothe a naked child, set aside grievances, or forgive a sharp word?

If we shared our lives with the same generosity and warmth as that with which Christmas gifts are given, we would be honoring Christ the entire year.

Prayer: Lord, help us to nourish the loving spirit we have shared with others this season, so it gives others happiness and serves You throughout the year. Amen.

THOUGHT FOR THE DAY
Hang on to the Christmas spirit.

~June M. Boone (Tennessee)

72   RESPONDING TO GOD
Read Amos 7:10-15

The LORD took me from following the flock, and the LORD said to me, "Go, prophesy."

—Amos 7:15 (RSV)

A YOUNG FRIEND WHO GRADUATED recently from university surprised me by informing me that she is going to study to be ordained as a minister. I knew her as a thoughtful, involved church member, but I had not suspected that her commitment went so deep. When I asked why she had decided on this course, she said, "Quite honestly, I don't feel that I made the decision myself."

It was enriching to hear a young person acknowledge so clearly that she was open to the guidance of God in her life, even though God led her into a path that she herself had not envisaged.

Long ago, such leading was experienced by the prophet Amos. Content in his calling as herdsman and dresser of fig trees, he nevertheless opened himself to being taken from his settled way of life because he felt the urgency of proclaiming the Lord's word.

Sometimes accepting God's guidance involves us in a course of action that we have not contemplated or particularly wanted. It may be inconvenient or even troublesome. True commitment leads to acting on what we feel to be God's will for us.

Prayer: God of the prophet Amos, help us to be always open to Your will and never to seek selfish excuses for avoiding it. Amen.

THOUGHT FOR THE DAY
Do we keep alert to recognize God's word?
~Jean Cameron Whiteford (Lanarkshire, Scotland)

73 SACRIFICE
Read Luke 9:18-27

[Jesus] said, "For those who want to save their life will lose it, and those who lose their life for my sake will save it."
—Luke 9:24 (NRSV)

JUNE 4, 1989 WAS A SHOCKING DAY in the history of China. That night, thousands of Chinese students and citizens who strived for freedom and democracy were killed by troops in Beijing, China. The incident was closely followed by arrest, imprisonment, and execution of many others.

I do not know how many of these people were Christians. However, I do know that without hesitation they sacrificed what is most precious—their blood and their lives—for their ideals.

How about us? We claim that we are Christian. But are we willing to sacrifice our efforts, wealth, time, love, and even our life for the truth and for the responsibilities that God has placed on us?

Prayer: Eternal God, please forgive us for our selfishness. Help us realize the true meaning of sacrifice. Enlighten us to discern Your opportunities for service to others. In Jesus' name. Amen.

THOUGHT FOR THE DAY
Where do I draw the line in my willingness to sacrifice for my faith?

~Chan Hing Fai (Hong Kong, China)

74 NEW FRIENDS
Read Matthew 25:31-40

And the King will answer them, "Truly I tell you, just as you did it to one of the least of these who are members of my family, you did it to me."
—Matthew 25:40 (NRSV)

As I came down the railway platform slowly, with my bag on my left shoulder, I saw a beggar playing with a stray dog at the corner of the last step. The beggar needed a friend and the dog, an owner. Now when I go for my walking exercises and bazaar work, I wrap a wheat bread for the dog and two slices of yeast bread with butter or jam for the beggar.

We three have become friends, and we are growing in love and fondness for one another. Each time I near the platform, I notice the dog wagging its tail and a smile creasing the face of the beggar. Leprosy has taken fingers from his hands, and the dog is lame. We three have one common characteristic: we cannot run. We share another characteristic: we love one another. When I see my friends, my heart warms, and I can walk faster than usual.

When we bestow God's love on others, we are blessed. The dog and the beggar are now friends. And I have two new friends.

Prayer: Dear Lord of all creation, help us to spread Your love to all people and creatures, regardless of caste, color, creed, or status. Bring all people to awareness of Your love and care. Amen.

THOUGHT FOR THE DAY
Who near me needs to see my expression of God's love?

~Charles S. Khiyalie (Uttar Pradesh, India)

75 COLOR BEAUTIFUL
Read Romans 12:4-18

Just as each of us has one body with many members, and these members do not all have the same function, so in Christ we who are many form one body, and each member belongs to all the others.

—Romans 12:4, 5 (NIV)

BEING A WIFE in an intercultural marriage and a parent of two bicultural children, I often receive comments from other parents about racial issues. At my daughter's swimming lesson, one mother commented to me, "I'm teaching my child not to see color. I'm teaching him to be color blind."

Her statement made me think. Of course I don't want my children to make assumptions about people because of the color of their skin, but I also don't want my children to ignore the differences between us and the culture of others. I want to teach my children to see color because that is part of what makes each of us unique.

God made each of us differently and beautifully. We can teach our children to value and accept our diversity as a part of the world that God created for us. Let us teach others how Jesus died to save us all, for though we come from different backgrounds, "we who are many form one body" in Christ.

Prayer: Dear God, teach us to see the beauty in each one of us. Please keep our hearts and minds focused on You. In Jesus' name. Amen.

THOUGHT FOR THE DAY
Each of us is lovingly made by God.
~Martha Bragg (Minnesota)

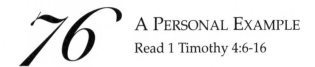

A PERSONAL EXAMPLE
Read 1 Timothy 4:6-16

[Paul wrote,] "Be imitators of me, as I am of Christ."
—1 Corinthians 11:1 (NRSV)

DURING THE LATTER DAYS of his life, my grandfather was almost deaf. To carry on a conversation with him, we had to shout.

But in spite of that he never missed a service of worship at church unless he was ill. One Sunday, a parishoner noticed that when Grandfather read the responsive reading he was a few words ahead or behind the congregation. After the service she asked him, "You don't hear much of what goes on in worship, do you? Why do you attend church Sunday after Sunday?"

"No," said my grandfather, "I don't hear much that is being said. But I believe I set an example for others. Those who attend can see that I am present. Just being in my pew is a witness to my Lord."

This is a valid witness to our Christian faith. We can always question a person's words, but we can never refute the witness of a person's life.

Prayer: Dear God, help us remember that wherever we are, others can see our actions. May our example encourage others to imitate us as we seek to imitate Christ. Amen.

THOUGHT FOR THE DAY
Part of serving God is being a good example.
~Lester L. Haws (California)

77 A New Life
Read Psalm 145:1-13

If anyone is in Christ, there is a new creation: everything old has passed away; see, everything has become new!
—2 Corinthians 5:17 (NRSV)

As a child, I attended a school run by Christian missionary sisters. There I learned about Jesus Christ. But the teachings made no perceptible impression on me at that time. Christianity was just another religion, one of the many religions practiced by the various races in Malaysia. Malaysia is a multiracial country where the people of each race usually follow the religious practices of their original homeland.

About two years ago, encouraged by a pastor friend, I accepted Christ as my Lord and Savior. From then on, my life began slowly but surely to change for the better in every way. Truly, God's promise to us of salvation and new life in Christ is glorious!

Today I live free from the miserable bondage to age-old superstitions and idolatrous practices of my past. Now I know for sure that Christianity is special. It grants me—and you—a joyous relationship with the living God, who loves us and steers us gently through both the good and bad in our lives.

Prayer: Dear God, we praise You for Your grace. We thank You that in Your great mercy You call each one of us to You. Amen.

Thought for the Day
New life in Christ is glorious!
~Lilian Leong Laylin (Penang, West Malaysia)

78 GOD WHO INTERVENES
Read Exodus 3:7-12

The Lord said, "I have seen the affliction of my people."
—Exodus 3:7 (RSV)

I WAS WATCHING A SWIMMING CLASS in progress. A few students were trying painstakingly to swim according to instructions from the coach, who was closely watching each one of his trainees in the pool. Suddenly I heard a splash, and I saw the coach swimming across, carrying one of his trainees who could swim no longer because of fatigue.

I then remembered what took place at Mount Horeb, when God spoke to Moses, "I have seen the affliction of my people . . . and have heard their cry because of their taskmasters; I know their sufferings, and I have come down to deliver them."

God is closely watching us in all our struggles and comes to us in the midst of our agony and suffering. God is no onlooker; God intervenes in history through people to deliver us from our bondages and alienations. It is God's leap into history that we see in Bethlehem's manger. And the message of God's kingdom which Jesus announced—good news to the poor—invites us to participate in the struggles of people to help release them from bondage.

Prayer: O God, we thank You for Your eternal vigil for us. Help us to break free from all fetters of bondage by relying on You. Make us instruments to free others. Amen.

THOUGHT FOR THE DAY
God frees us to free others.
~Joseph Ayrookuzhy (Kerala, India)

79   FORGETTING TO REMEMBER
Read Hebrews 13:15-16

I was hungry and you gave me food.
    —Matthew 25:35 (RSV)

ONE DAY LAST WINTER I stayed home from work to be with our 11-year-old son who had the flu. As he was napping, I decided to catch up on some long overdue household chores. As I was mopping the kitchen floor, I had to slide out a small kitchen cabinet. In doing so, I noticed something sticking out behind it—a brown grocery bag, folded flat and neat, with a shopping list stapled to it. This was not just any shopping list—it was marked "URGENT" across the top in bold black letters. Beneath that were Jesus' words from Matthew quoted above.

This bag was from our church. I was to have filled it with groceries for the needy and taken it to our local urban ministry. I felt a rush of guilt as I pulled it out and dusted away the cobwebs. How long had it been there? Had a family done without much-needed food that week because of my neglect? Had they suffered because I was too busy or forgetful? And most of all, why did I need such a tangible reminder to do what God expects me to do as a matter of course in my Christian life?

God never forgets us. May I always remember those who need me.

Prayer: Lord, let us never forget to provide for the hungry and those in need. In Jesus' name. Amen.

THOUGHT FOR THE DAY
As God remembers our needs, so should we remember the needs of those around us.
    ~Cheryl Weekley Mays (Georgia)

80 So Near Yet So Far

Read Ephesians 2:13-22

You are no longer strangers and sojourners, but you are fellow citizens with the saints and members of the household of God.
—Ephesians 2:19 (RSV)

RECENTLY, A DELEGATION from the churches in Thailand visited the churches in Burma, our next-door neighbor. After returning they gave a report about the Burmese churches which have been isolated for many years. They told of the warm, Christian fellowship they experienced with Burmese Christians.

A Burmese woman in the audience then sang for us a song about December and January. These two months stand next to each other, but on the calendar they are also far from each other. We all realized the point: though we are Christians living in countries which are next-door neighbors, we are far apart.

Very often Christians do not realize that through Christ we are one. Even if we live far apart, we are fellow citizens of the household of God. When we allow divisions such as race and denomination to exist, we stay far from each other when we could be near.

Prayer: Father, forgive us our sins that separate us from Thee and from other believers. Help us to overcome our differences and become instruments for peace and understanding. We pray through Christ, who has made us one. Amen.

THOUGHT FOR THE DAY
Christ brings together those who are far apart.
~Pornwadee Arkkapin (Bangkok, Thailand)

GRATEFUL
HEARTS

81   GRATEFULNESS
Read 1 Thessalonians 5:12-24

Be thankful in all circumstances. This is what God wants from you in your life in union with Christ Jesus.
—1 Thessalonians 5:18 (TEV)

THE SECOND GRADERS LINED UP to go home for Christmas vacation, clutching the small gifts they had been asked to open at home. A few mumbled, "Thank you," or asked, "What is it?" But there were a couple of candid children in the bunch.

"If I don't like it, I'm going to give it to my sister," Melvin said.

"Teacher, I'll like it," Johnny said. "Even if it's under-wear, I'll like it."

I've often thought how many times our responses are more like Melvin's than Johnny's. Melvin made it plain that he would reject the gift if it was not to his liking. How many times do we ask the Lord to order our days and then fuss and fume when things don't go just the way we wanted?

The last thing a second grader would want is under-wear—yet Johnny was grateful even for that. How many times are we grateful for the practical things God does in our lives that are not necessarily fun but are essential for us to grow?

Which response blesses the giver?

Prayer: God, help me be grateful for all Your gifts—not just the ones I think I want. Amen.

THOUGHT FOR THE DAY
God's gifts meet our needs as well as our wants.

~Nan Jordan (Georgia)

82 A Gift for Jamie

Read Matthew 6:25-34

Every good gift and every perfect gift is from above.
—James 1:17 (KJV)

ONE CHRISTMAS when I was a child, money was scarce. My father had been injured in a mine accident, and his compensation checks were long overdue. He faced Christmas with worry in his eyes, and soon a heavy cloud hung over our family.

The day before Christmas, we visited my grandmother. When we returned home, we found a young boy in our living room, staring wide-eyed at our Christmas tree.

As we looked at Jamie and saw the joy and wonder he felt because of our tree, each of us saw how beautiful it really was and how fortunate we all were. We had each other, a warm home, enough to eat—and Christmas. Sometimes we cannot see our blessings because we focus on obstacles. Other times we take things for granted and miss the joy of gratefulness.

Prayer: Dear God, help us to focus on our blessings and give You our worries. We pray as Jesus taught, "Our Father in heaven, hallowed be your Name, your kingdom come, your will be done, on earth as in heaven. Give us today our daily bread. Forgive us our sins as we forgive those who sin against us. Save us from the time of trial, and deliver us from evil. For the kingdom, the power, and the glory are yours, now and for ever. Amen."*

THOUGHT FOR THE DAY
God's gift of love is for sharing.
~Linda Cherry (Ontario, Canada)

---

*From *Prayers We Have in Common* © 1970, 1971, and 1975, International Consultation on English Texts.

83 ALL YEAR LONG
Read John 15:12-17

Jesus said, "This is my commandment, that you love one another as I have loved you."
—John 15:12 (RSV)

ON TOP OF MY LIST of New Year's resolutions I put "Thank-you notes for Christmas." It is important to tell others we appreciate their love shown through their gifts.

We recently received one such delightful note for the Christmas loaf we gave. Not only did the woman thank us for remembering her, but she added a special touch that sums up the meaning of Christmas for me. She wrote, "I plan to pass the lovely thought on by making a cream cheese sandwich with the loaf and taking some of it to a neighbor who is ill. We will break bread together and remember you." If we all could pass on the love of Christmas to others well into the new year, what a wonderful winter it would be for everyone!

Epiphany reminds us that God's loving presence shown clearly at Christmas continues beyond Christmas. Somehow as Christmas recedes into our memories and we no longer hear the carols, it is difficult to remember that. We must work doubly hard to bring the spirit of love to Groundhog Day or May Day or even August 21st! The real meaning of Christmas depends on our love being passed on to others 365 days a year.

Prayer: Remind us, dear God, that as Your love for us is constant, so You expect our love for others to be. May we keep the spirit of Christmas throughout the year. Amen.

THOUGHT FOR THE DAY
God's love is never out of season.
~W. Stanley Smith (North Carolina)

84

A Promise Fulfilled
Read Luke 2:22-40

Simeon prayed, "Mine eyes have seen thy salvation which thou hast prepared in the presence of all peoples."
—Luke 2:30-31 (RSV)

I HAVE ALWAYS LIKED THE STORY of Simeon and Anna. Here are two elderly people who have been consistent for many years with their prayers, fasting, and worship. They have believed in God's promise of a messiah and have done everything to prepare themselves for His coming.

Now the moment arrives when the Child is presented at the temple. Anna is already there, and Simeon is "inspired by the Spirit" to come into the temple.

Because of their expectation and preparation, Simeon and Anna recognize the fulfillment of God's promise in this child Jesus. Better yet, their recognition leads to praise and thanksgiving to God for a promised fulfilled.

Prayer: Dear God, we thank You for the example of Simeon and Anna, whose lives portrayed steadfastness of faith and confidence in Your promises. Help us follow their example so that we will be ready too. "Our Father, who art in heaven, hallowed be thy Name. Thy kingdom come. Thy will be done, on earth as it is in heaven. Give us this day our daily bread. And forgive us our trespasses, as we forgive those who trespass against us. And lead us not into temptation, but deliver us from evil. For thine is the kingdom, and the power, and the glory, for ever and ever. Amen."

THOUGHT FOR THE DAY

Am I prepared to recognize Jesus when He comes to me?

~Mary Eleanore James (California)

85

A GLOOMY DAY?
Read Genesis 1:26-31

The earth is the LORD'S, and the fulness thereof; the world, and they that dwell therein.

—Psalm 24:1 (KJV)

IT WAS A COLD, RAINY DAY in December, one of a series of gloomy days when it seemed the sun would never shine again. I bundled up to walk the long driveway to the mailbox, hoping for a newsy letter or a colorful magazine to brighten the day. But the mailbox was empty.

As I started back to the house, I became aware that a bluebird was accompanying me. The bird would sit on a fence post until I drew near. Then it would rise into the air, flutter its wings, trill a few cheery notes, and fly on to the next post. In this manner the bird stayed close to me all the way to the house. I forgot the cold and gloom and slowed my steps to prolong the enjoyment. I wondered if this friendly creature knew that I am the one who fills the bird feeder every day. Or was the bird just curious about me, a strange creature who was invading its territory?

No matter. I felt I was privileged to witness one of God's miracles. I said a silent prayer of thanks that humankind is taking steps to preserve life on this earth, from the smallest and most insignificant to the largest and most awe-inspiring forms of life. Suddenly, I realized that it was a beautiful day after all.

Prayer: Thank You, Father, for this earth You have given us to enjoy and to maintain. Help us to see beauty in each day. Amen.

THOUGHT FOR THE DAY
Do something every day to preserve the earth.

~Anna S. Murrell (Tennessee)

86   IN THE FOLDS OF GOD'S GARMENT

Read 1 Samuel 25:23-31 and
Malachi 3:16–4:3

Abigail said to David, "Even though someone is pursuing you to take your life, the life of my master will be bound securely in the bundle of the living by the LORD your God."
—1 Samuel 25:29 (NIV)

IN CHITTAGONG, BANGLADESH, on the other side of the world from my boyhood home, I waited while an old man tugged at the knot in the waist of his faded lunghi (a one-piece, skirt-like garment for men). It reminded me of my mother's tying a few coins into the corner of my handkerchief when I was a small boy. The old man's gnarled fingers worked until the knot was loosened. Out came some small coins, a tiny box of wooden matches, and two old, rusty keys. These were his treasures.

In ancient Palestine the fold of a garment was used in the same fashion. When Abigail blessed David she shared with him a tender picture of God's care. The old man on the streets of Chittagong helped me to understand what Abigail meant and what David understood.

The Revised English Bible makes the picture explicit: "The LORD your God will wrap your life up and put it with his own treasure." We are God's treasure. God cares for us and keeps us close as though in the folds of God's own garment.

Prayer: O Lord God, thank You for caring for me. Help me to realize my worth to You and the worth of those around me. Amen.

THOUGHT FOR THE DAY
I am one of God's treasures.
~William D. Barrick (Chittagong, Bangladesh)

87 AND IT WAS GOOD
Read Genesis 1

God saw all that he had made, and it was very good.
—Genesis 1:31 (NIV)

As we watched through our kitchen window, the garbage truck rumbled its noisy way down the street while the two collectors worked opposite sides of the street. In the process, one man dropped some cans and papers in the middle of the road. He kept going, and within seconds the wind began to scatter the debris.

As the other collector emptied our pails into the truck, a few bits of paper fell near the side of the road. Swiftly stopping down, he grabbed the litter and tossed it into the truck.

Probably nobody except us had seen what the second man had done, but then we have seen him act this way before—many times. He consistently takes time to get rid of the clutter in whatever little part of the world he happens to be. Woven into his ordinary actions is a basic reverence for creation. Someone whose name we do not even know and whom we have seen only at a distance continues to help us reflect on how we treat our surroundings and the world our Creator has given us.

Prayer: The beauties of Your creation surround us, Lord. May we treat the works of Your hands with ever-deepening gratitude and reverence for their sacredness. Amen.

THOUGHT FOR THE DAY

The way we treat creation reveals our attitude toward the Creator.

~John and Patricia Brewster (New York)

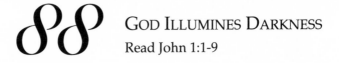 God Illumines Darkness
Read John 1:1-9

Thou art my lamp, O LORD; And the LORD illumines my darkness.

—2 Samuel 22:29 (NASB)

ONE RAINY DAY when I was twelve, I had to help bring our buffaloes home from the jungle. Since the sun could not be seen at this time of the year due to rain and dark clouds, it was hard to tell night from day in the jungle.

I led a boy and a girl to chase the herd home. We came to a big lake surrounded by forest, and half the buffaloes slipped into the water. The others rested on the ground as if to spend the night. No amount of shouting and beating would move them.

Suddenly I saw glowworms flying about us, and I realized that night had come. We were still far from the village. Fear seized me. At that moment heavy rain poured down. I decided to leave the animals there. I started praying aloud, "God, please save us." Suddenly, the rain stopped and we saw the sky. We thanked God.

After a hard struggle through the tall grasses and trees, we reached the top of a mountain. From there we could see the village. I called out loudly for my mother, and she responded from a distance. She came with an elder of the village, bringing a lantern to guide us home. The inner light in my heart was stronger than the darkness that surrounded us.

Prayer: O Lord, help us to see our way even when we are in darkness. Amen.

THOUGHT FOR THE DAY
God searches for us when we are in darkness.

~D. Singson (Manipur, India)

EVERY GOOD DAY
Read Psalm 118:19-29

This is the day that the LORD has made; let us rejoice and be glad in it.

—Psalm 118:24 (NRSV)

OUR FIVE-YEAR-OLD DAUGHTER begins her bedtime prayer each night with, "Thank You, God, for this beautiful day," no matter how rainy, cold, or dreary that particular day may have been. I smile to myself, remembering the flooded creek waters rushing over the driveway or the sun never peeking through the gloomy clouds the entire day.

A few days ago we were traveling in the car when suddenly she began to explain to me why her prayers always begin in this way. She said, "It is because God made it and gave it all to me."

I am amazed at her insight and sense of gratitude. How wonderful to be reminded of the splendor that each day presents to us! Each day has its own glory that is much more than the weather conditions outside our window. It is a gift that God makes and gives to us. How can we do any less than be thankful for it?

Prayer: Dear Lord, help us to see the beauty of each day You have given us, that we may glorify You. We pray as Your children, saying, "Our Father which art in heaven, Hallowed be thy name. Thy kingdom come. Thy will be done in earth, as it is in heaven. Give us this day our daily bread. And forgive us our debts, as we forgive our debtors. And lead us not into temptation, but deliver us from evil: For thine is the kingdom, and the power, and the glory, for ever. Amen."*

THOUGHT FOR THE DAY
God makes each day and gives it to us.
~Rosalynde J. Robertson (Virginia)

*Matthew 6:9-13 (KJV).

90

PEAR TREES
Read 1 Corinthians 4:1-7

Didn't God give you everything you have?
—1 Corinthians 4:7 (TEV)

THE PEAR TREES ARE JUST THERE. No consequence or result of my sweat. They came with the house, stuck on the outer limits of the property, and were hardly noticeable when we moved in. But now their fruit is magnificent—bigger than a large man's fist, sun-splashed with ruby and amber hues. Not a worm, insect, or disease is to be found among them. They are just there.

So what do I do with free fruit from two trees? I could eat the pears right off the branches. I could can them for winter eating. I could bake pear pies, pear cobbler, and pear dumplings. I might prepare gallons of pear relish or large quantities of pear jelly. Yes, all that. As I reflected on this unexpected gift, I began to admire, appreciate, and meditate on the mysteries of God—the undeserved grace of God, the unselfish goodness of God. Reflecting on this gift of fruit causes me to say, "Thank You, Lord," for other gifts I have received: health, life, children, friends, and a spiritual inheritance.

Prayer: All-caring, all-providing God, help me to be a thankful, faithful manager of all Your precious gifts, sharing them with others and giving You the credit. In Jesus' name. Amen.

THOUGHT FOR THE DAY
How many of my most cherished possessions have been given to me?

~James K. Wagner (Ohio)

NEW
BEGINNINGS

91 A New Beginning
Read Ephesians 4:17-24

To him who is able to keep you from falling and to present you before his glorious presence without fault and with great joy— to the only God our Savior be glory.

—Jude 24, 25 (NIV)

A BROAD EXPANSE of glistening white sand spread out to meet the creamy foam created by breakers crashing onto the shore. Bright morning sunshine, cloudless blue sky, and sparkling azure sea made a glorious picture. I stood and gazed out over one of Australia's many beaches. The sand was smooth and unmarked as it curved around the bay and stretched off into the distance.

Before long, crowds of holiday makers began to arrive. By afternoon the sand was covered with footprints, broken-down sand castles, and people with their assorted belongings. But later in the evening, the tide came in. Water washed over the sand and then slowly receded, and the beach was again clean and smooth.

Seeing this made me think of how God works in our lives. God can change us and make us new persons with the chance to start fresh. If we confess our sins and are truly sorry, God forgives us; and it is as if we had never sinned. Like the sand on the beach, we are restored and stand before God without fault.

Prayer: Heavenly Father, forgive us for the sins that have marred our lives. Cleanse us and help us to begin again. Amen.

THOUGHT FOR THE DAY
I can start again.
~Norma Dawson (New South Wales, Australia)

92 A CONSTANT LOVE
Read Philippians 4:4-9

Rejoice in the Lord always; again I will say, Rejoice.
—Philippians 4:4 (RSV)

I SLUMPED IN THE CHURCH PEW with an exhausted sigh. For weeks I had been caught up in the whirlwind of the holidays—exchanging gifts, baking, washing, cleaning, visiting. But now, at last, the Sunday after New Year's Day, Christmas was finally over.

Yet as I relaxed to the organ prelude, I noticed that the Christmas tree was still standing in the corner. Candles still glowed from the altar and the Advent wreath. I stood up with the congregation to sing *We Three Kings* and *Silent Night*, and lay leaders read verses about the adoration of the Magi. As I took Communion, surrounded by the love of my husband and members of the congregation, I realized that Christmas was not over.

Christmas does not end on December 26 or on New Year's Eve. The excitement and bustle end, but the true celebration of Christ's presence in the world is not limited to a special day or season. His constant love is there for us day after day, year after year. I left the sanctuary renewed in the Christmas—and Christian—spirit of love and hope.

Prayer: Dear Lord, let me always remember that You are there for me, giving me love and strength on holidays, on workdays, on all my days. Amen.

THOUGHT FOR THE DAY
God's love is not seasonal.
~Jean Knight (California)

93   STOCKTAKING
Read Psalm 103:1-14

In everything God works for good with those who love him.
—Romans 8:28 (RSV)

IT CAN BE A GOOD PRACTICE to take stock, so to speak, of our life at the end of a year. One year, I set a time apart to consider what the year had meant for me. I relived so many blessings poured upon me by my Creator during the twelve months—professional, familial, and spiritual—that in the depth of my heart I said as the psalmist, "Bless the Lord, O my soul; and all that is within me, bless his holy name!"

On the other hand, I remembered serious difficulties which could have become lasting sources of sorrow. But those problems seemed very small in the light of the blessings I had enjoyed. Later they were happily solved.

This taking stock made me freshly aware of the certainty of Christ's promise, "I will be with you always."

God has continued faithful, and this has empowered me to start the new year with full confidence in God's loving concern.

Prayer: Grant us, O God, the grace of pausing to count Your blessings. May this result in gratitude to You and in consecration of our entire lives to Your service. Through Christ Jesus our Lord. Amen.

THOUGHT FOR THE DAY
Counting God's blessings leaves little time for lamenting.

~Marco Depestre, Jr. (Petit-Goave, Haiti)

94 FRESH EVERY MORNING
Read Lamentations 3:22-36

[Jesus said,] "The one who believes in me will also do the works that I do and in fact, will do greater works than these, because I am going to the Father."

—John 14:12 (NRSV)

"ANOTHER YEAR GONE," we say with a reflective sigh. Then we feel a twinge of anxiety about the year to come. We may feel safer with the familiar past, no matter how terrible it may have been, than with the unknown future.

But as Christians our attitude can be different. We can be grateful for the past but not sad at its departure. All that was good in the past we have enjoyed. All that was sad we have endured. That God's power has blessed us in both circumstances and will surely lead us on can give us peace and hope.

Our God is not God only of the past. God is God also of the present and of the living. God speaks to us in the present. And our loving Lord has even better things to give us tomorrow than what came to us yesterday or today. God loves us and also relies upon us, and with the Holy Spirit's power we will do even greater things than Jesus did. What an amazing statement! And what reassurance!

Prayer: O Lord, we take You at Your word. We believe that You have even greater things in store for us than in the past. Let us be reassured of Your love. Amen.

THOUGHT FOR THE DAY
If we believe, we will see the mighty outpouring of the power of the Lord!

~Ignatius S. Pinto (Bangalore, India)

95

NEWNESS OF LIFE
Read 2 Corinthians 5:11-19

If anyone is in Christ, there is a new creation: everything old had passed away; see, everything has become new!
—2 Corinthians 5:17 (NRSV)

IN BOMBAY, INDIA, there is an ancient custom of burning effigies on the last day of the year to wipe away the tragedies and disappointments of the past year as a new year is begun. The Germans burn fireworks to frighten away the evil spirits which lurk in the vicinity. Spaniards gather at midnight in the Puerta del Sol in Madrid. As the old clock strikes midnight, each person eats a grape with each strike, believing this brings luck for the new year.

Many people in France and Scandinavia burn yule logs cut from fruit trees to bring a good harvest in the year to come. All of these customs illustrate the need people feel for a fresh start in their lives.

The fresh start Paul speaks of, however, is different from these kinds of traditions. When a person accepts Jesus as Savior, that person becomes a new being. Past sins and misdeeds are forgotten. Whether this happens in the middle of the year or at its end, God gives that person a new heart and a new spirit.

Prayer: God of all time, we commit ourselves to Thee at the beginning of the new year. Fill us with Thy spirit that we may walk in newness of life. Amen.

THOUGHT FOR THE DAY
In the new year I will walk with renewed faith.
~Sarojini Martin (Frankfurt, Germany)

96 WHAT YOU DO WELL
Read 1 Samuel 2:18-20

[Samuel's] mother used to make for him a little robe and take it to him each year.

—1 Samuel 2:19 (RSV)

NATE SAINT FELT CALLED to the mission field. But he lacked the usual missionary skills. When he discovered a need for missionary pilots, he was overjoyed. He could bring to the Lord the thing he loved to do best—flying. Nate died a martyr's death in the Ecuadorian jungle, but his life is an inspiration to others who desire to bring to the Lord what they enjoy doing well.

Hannah was limited in what she could do for her son Samuel after she brought him to the tabernacle at Shiloh. But she found what she did well and brought him what she could—clothing she had made.

Many of us lack skills in church leadership, in teaching or preaching. Many of us, like Hannah, lack opportunities for what we consider major service. But we do some things well. Perhaps it is cooking, sewing, crafts, carpentry, mechanics, reading, gardening. By sharing our skills and the products of our labor with others, we can witness to the love of Christ. God can use what we love to do best.

Prayer: Creator God, help us to discover ways of giving to You what we do best. Amen.

THOUGHT FOR THE DAY
God takes pleasure in our abilities.
~Wanda M. Trawick (South Carolina)

97

ON LOSING CHRIST
Read Luke 2:41-52

Supposing [Jesus] to be in the company they went a day's journey. . . . and when they did not find him, they returned to Jerusalem, seeking him.

—Luke 2:44-45 (RSV)

IT IS A SAD THING TO HAVE CHRIST, then lose him. Like Mary and Joseph, we can easily lose Christ amid the ceaseless round of everyday activities. But how?

1. We can lose Christ by giving our attention to secondary considerations. Am I putting Christ first in my life? Jesus said we are to seek first the kingdom of God and God's righteousness.

2. We can lose Christ in the liturgy and forms of worship that are meant to reveal Him to us. In worship, is my attention centered on the presence of Christ? Or is my faith more form than substance?

3. We can lose Christ in negative personal relationships. It is easy to love those who love us. But do we show love and forgiveness to those who have injured us or mistreated us? The Bible challenges us, "Forgive . . . as God has forgiven you."

Much of life's joy lies in mutual discovery of Christ with our brothers and sisters. And having found Christ, may we share His love.

Prayer: God of us all, be with all who earnestly seek for truth. May we truly find You and having found You, spend our lives in love and service to others. Amen.

THOUGHT FOR THE DAY
I will seek Christ amid today's activities.
~Richard W. Thomas (Ohio)

GROWING PAINS
Read Philippians 2:12-16

It is God which worketh in you both to will and to do of his good pleasure.
—Philippians 2:13 (KJV)

MY FATHER AND I SAT in his sun-drenched pasture watching a cow tend her newborn calf. First she carefully bathed it with her tongue. Then she firmly nudged the wet, scrawny creature with her nose.

"What is she doing," I asked. "Won't she hurt it?"

"Oh, no," Daddy said. "She is encouraging the calf to stand on its feet so it will develop properly."

The mother nudged this way and that, flopping her offspring over. Finally the calf wobbled to its feet, only to crash nose first to the ground, legs spread-eagled. Again and again it tried. Then came the moment of victory. The shaky calf stood and took its first clumsy steps.

The incident reminded me of the first weeks after I became a Christian. I wanted to bask in the wonder of this new experience. Instead, God began nudging me to walk in new paths of service.

Many times I felt inadequate, insecure. Sometimes I fell on my face in my efforts to work and witness. Yet the new birth is not an end in itself. It is only the beginning of a lifelong growth process.

Prayer: Lord, help me to be sensitive to new opportunities for growth and service. Amen.

THOUGHT FOR THE DAY
God continually nudges us toward growth.
~Gayle Martin Pruitt (South Carolina)

99 JOURNEYS OF FAITH
Read Genesis 12:1-7

The LORD said to Abram, "Go from your country . . . to the land that I will show you."

—Genesis 12:1 (RSV)

LIKE ABRAHAM, FAITH JOURNEYERS are sustained by the recognition of a divine relationship. Abraham knew that One with a purpose was walking beside him. He had a sense of sufficiency for whatever life would bring.

It is false to think that a smooth life is the best life. That kind of life may never motivate us to seek God's will. We are given strength to bear burdens in the course of moving toward the goal that God wants us to reach.

Abraham was open to change. He had been cultivating the attitude that makes ultimate ventures possible. The truth of God's leading would be revealed only in Abraham's willingness to act.

Though Abraham could not see the end of his journey, he had the courage to begin. God asks of us not promises that we can go a long way but humble obedience that makes a start in the right direction.

Prayer: O God, don't let our best ambitions stop short in moral compromise. We pray, "Our Father which art in heaven, Hallowed be thy name. Thy kingdom come. Thy will be done in earth, as it is in heaven. Give us this day our daily bread. And forgive us our debts, as we forgive our debtors. And lead us not into temptation, but deliver us from evil: For thine is the kingdom, and the power, and the glory, for ever. Amen."*

THOUGHT FOR THE DAY
Am I open to change?

~Charles E. Link (California)

*Matthew 6:9-13 (KJV).

100 BEGINNING WITH FAITH
Read Genesis 12:1-9

By faith [Abraham] sojourned in the land of promise.
—Hebrews 11:9 (RSV)

ABRAHAM WAS CALLED BY GOD to leave behind his life in Ur and go into a land he knew nothing about. Abraham had no idea what would befall him, but he went on faith, believing that God would be faithful to him. Because Abraham believed in the faithfulness of God, Abraham kept faith with God.

We are entering a new year. God is calling us to turn from the past to an unknown future. God is calling us to a task though we do not know what lies ahead. We may make plans, dream dreams, and set goals—and everything may turn out as we expect. But it may not. God is calling us into that uncertain future and saying, "I want you to get up and go. I will be with you. If you will be obedient to my commands and trust me to lead you into the uncharted future, your life will be rewarding and fruitful."

The new year is an opportunity for a new beginning with God—to love and care about the things God cares about. What an exciting time lies ahead for those who walk by faith with God!

Prayer: Dear God, thank You for calling us to discipleship and for the opportunity to love and serve You. Help us overcome those things that hinder a life of joy and fruitful work with You. Amen.

THOUGHT FOR THE DAY
The joy of living is walking by faith.
~James W. Simmons (Indiana)